This book is dedicated to everybody who contributed to this incredible restoration project, especially those who put in countless hours doing all the unglamorous bits and pieces - like the inventive metalwork, removing rust and old paint, solving unsolvable problems, and of course the blood, sweat and tears that are spent in seeing it through to completion.

Without the relentless effort put in by Ruth and Keith Andrews in driving this project since 2007, it would have been unlikely to reach its triumphant conclusion.

They were ably supported by many people, but especially Norman Aish, whose ability to find replacement parts and clever people to deal with problems never failed, and Bob Smith who, time and again, used his technical expertise in sorting the mechanical issues.

FRIENDS OF KING ALFRED BUSES

THE RETURN OF THE OLYMPIC

told by
Stephen Morris

with extra material from
James Freeman
Ruth & Keith Andrews

designed & produced by
Ray Stenning of Best Impressions

for
Friends of King Alfred Buses

printed by
Rusper Print Ltd

published by
Best Impressions
15 Starfield Road
London W12 9SN

copyright ©
Stephen Morris &
Friends of King Alfred Buses

a superb **Classic Bus** production

ISBN 978 0 9565740 1 5

THE KING IS DEAD, LONG LIVE THE KING

Under the watchful gaze of Sir Hamo Thornycroft's imposing statue of King Alfred, erected in 1901, three buses from the fleet of King Alfred Motor Services await departure from Winchester's Broadway in the early 1960s. This is where almost all King Alfred services began and ended their journeys.

The two double deckers are Leyland bodied Leyland Titans, highbridge HAA 809 leading and lowbridge KOR 382 behind.

The single decker is Leyland Olympic JAA 708, the star of this book.

There's an interesting collection of cars parked in the centre of the Broadway, too, including the drophead Sunbeam-Talbot nearest the camera.

There is a considerable interest in the heritage of Britain's buses. Quite rightly; the ability for large numbers of people to be able to enjoy mobility has shaped the way we as Britons live and has been a major influence on the way towns and cities developed over the 20th century.

Winchester's transport heritage is especially well preserved, thanks to the efforts of a small group of volunteers, the Friends of King Alfred Buses, to save every known example of the bus fleet of the small yet distinctive company which served the city for more than 50 years. King Alfred Motor Services, run by the Chisnell family, ran local bus services in and around the city from 1922 until its larger neighbour Hants & Dorset took over its operations: King Alfred's last bus ran on 28 April 1973.

FoKAB's quest to find as many King Alfred buses as possible has taken them to the USA, and to Ireland: in 1990 a significant bus, thought to have been destroyed by fire, was finally repatriated. This was a bus that had been responsible - literally - for changing the shape of Winchester's buses in 1950.

The restoration of this bus has been an epic task, and as a result of the significance of the bus and the size of the restoration task, its progress was followed by Bus & Coach Preservation magazine. This book uses these articles as a basis to tell the story of a task many thought impossible: the restoration of 1950 Leyland Olympic JAA 708.

THE OLYMPIC
A NEW BUS FOR A NEW ERA

FoKAB's Olympic is a significant vehicle in a number of respects. It entered service with King Alfred Motor Services in October 1950 as the first underfloor-engined bus in Winchester. This was a fascinating period in British automotive history: development of new models had almost ground to a halt during the war and the 1948-1950 period particularly saw a rash of new models, cars as well as buses, that would begin to change the face of Britain's roads. Few were more radical than the new underfloor-engined buses that gave greater capacity and immediately made traditional halfcab single-deckers look dated.

The Olympic, Leyland's first postwar sortie into underfloor-engined buses, was announced in 1949, in a 27ft 6in by 7ft 6in 40-seat form, the HR40. But the major advantage of the underfloor engine was that it enabled more seats to be fitted, and so when regulations were relaxed in 1951 to allow 30ft by 8ft single-deckers on two axles, the 30ft long 44-seat HR44 was to become more popular. After all there was little point in accepting the additional complexity and expense of such a design if you didn't maximise the benefits of its capacity. Only 19 HR40s were built. Five went to Birmingham and eight to Isle of Man Road Services, and the rest went to smaller operators.

There was more to the Olympic than just the shape of the bus. Under the skin the whole approach represented radical engineering: described as integral, the bus was conceived and built as a single unit, rather than the traditional way of building buses, as a separate chassis on to which people with cabinet-making or metal-working skills could build a structure in which passengers could sit.

In today's terms the Olympic may be better described as 'integrated' rather than 'integral'; unlike the later Routemaster which was a monocoque construction from which mechanical components were hung, the Olympic effectively has a separate chassis, but the body is engineered as part of a single structure of which that chassis is a part, eliminating the need for a separate body bearer and thereby reducing overall weight. Sixty years on, it's a technique used by many modern buses, whereby the body structure is properly engineered in conjunction with the underframe. In the case of the Olympic engineering techniques used for building aircraft were adapted to the bus, and some components were built using aircraft materials, not least Duralumin, the aluminium alloy used for panelling.

It's this combination of a heavy steel underframe and aluminium that have made the survival of JAA 708 possible: much of the steel structure has had to be replaced, but the heavy underframe, aluminium panelling and aluminium pillars have survived well, and most of what you will see as the completed bus will be original material, even if much of the steelwork behind the panels is new. The bus was exported to Ireland in 1966 and withdrawn from service in 1975; it was

Announcing
THE NEW Leyland
M·C·W
"OLYMPIC"

MAXIMUM SEATING CAPACITY
UNDER-FLOOR ENGINE BUS
OF INTEGRAL CONSTRUCTION

Lighter & Stronger · built to last longer

Manufactured by

LEYLAND MOTORS LIMITED
Head Office and Works
LEYLAND · LANCASHIRE · ENGLAND

METROPOLITAN-CAMMELL-WEYMANN MOTOR BODIES Ltd.
VICKERS HOUSE · BROADWAY · WESTMINSTER · ENGLAND

thought to have been lost but, in actual fact, it languished in a field until rediscovered and repatriated in 1990. It could easily have rotted away beyond the state of being salvaged in that time, but for its unusual style of construction.

FoKAB's Chris Kent has fond memories of travelling home from school on the Olympic in the early-1950s, and has had much to do with its restoration, although he spends much of his time in the West Country and doesn't get to Winchester quite as often as he would like now. He recalls how the bus was driven by King Alfred's top driver, who usually drove Leyland Tiger coaches but would fill in a schools duty with the Olympic between coach jobs. With its 125bhp Leyland O.600 engine it was very fast, he remembers: rather over-engined for a bus only 27ft 6in long: and other drivers were rather afraid of it. Indeed when new it was fitted with vacuum brakes, but was very soon converted to air brakes, presumably more in keeping with its performance, though still something of a novelty on a provincial motorbus at the time.

JAA 708 is one of only two surviving HR40s - the other is from the Isle of Man - and one of only four UK-spec Olympics remaining: the other two are HR44s of Jennings of Ashen and Ribble.

On the opposite page is a contemporary trade press advert for the new Olympic; also its distinctive front badge, while on this page is a technical drawing of the bus. Note that the side window ventilators on JAA 708 differ from those on the advert and this drawing; also there is no nearside mirror - these were still considered frivolous in 1950.

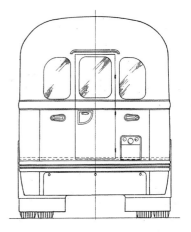

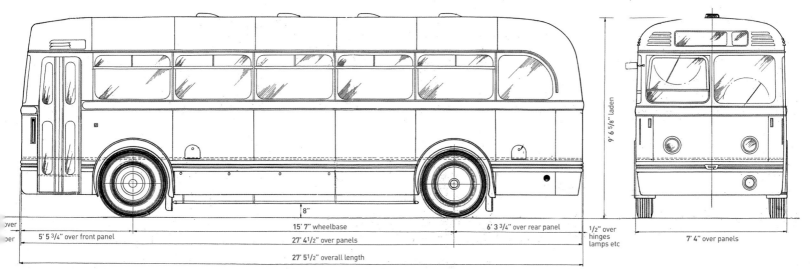

9' 6 5/8" laden

8"

over

ber

5' 5 3/4" over front panel

15' 7" wheelbase

27' 4½" over panels

6' 3¾" over rear panel

27' 5½" overall length

1/2" over hinges lamps etc

7' 4" over panels

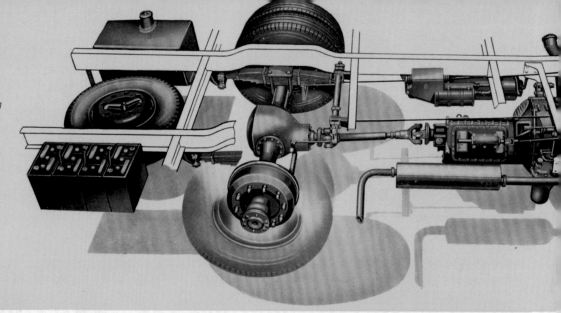

This charming spread is taken from the sales brochure produced by Leyland for the Olympic when it was first introduced. It's nice to imagine Mr Bob Chisnell with his brother Fred, joint proprietors of King Alfred Motor Services, poring over its pages while deciding whether to place their order for this revolutionary machine.

POWER UNITS Engine and gearbox of unit construction flexibly mounted amidships under the floor by Leyland link mounting. Overall depth of unit 22 in. Parts requiring inspection, such as injection pump, injectors, tappets, fuel and oil filters, dipstick and oil filler etc., are accessible through hinged valances.

ENGINE Leyland 6-cylinder direct-injection diesel. Bore and stroke, 4·8 in. × 5·5 in. (122 mm. × 139·7 mm.) ; Cubic capacity 597 cu. in. (9·8 litres) ; Brake horse power 125/130 b.h.p. (127 metric b.h.p.) at 1800 r.p.m. ; Maximum Torque, 410 lb. ft. (56·7 Kg.-M.)

at 900 r.p.m. ; Fuel consumption, minimum 0.34 pts./b.h.p./hr. (162·8 grm./h.p./hr.), maximum 0·36 pts./b.h.p./hr. (172 grm./h.p./hr.) ;
Monobloc-cast cylinder block and crankcase with renewable pre-finished dry liners ; valve seats and valves stellite-faced ; 7-bearing nitrided crankshaft ; copper-lead strip bearings ; 5-ring aluminium pistons ; helical-toothed timing gear ; 7-bearing camshaft in crankcase ; lubrication via full-flow external filter ; pressure to main, big-end, camshaft and timing gear bearings.

ENGINE AUXILIARIES Injection pump on left side and compressor at left front driven from timing gear ; starter at left rear, 7-in. dynamo located forward of engine and belt driven from fan drive ; oil-bath air cleaner.

FUEL SYSTEM Leyland multi-hole nozzles with edge-trap filters; C.A.V. injection pump with patent Leyland mechanical and vacuum governor ; diaphragm-type lift-pump ; 50 gallon tank.

COOLING SYSTEM Self-adjusting pump; thermostat controlled circulation ; flat tube type radiator located amidships with 19 in. close-cowled 4-bladed fan driven from forward end of crankshaft.

CLUTCH Single-plate dry type, 16¼ in. dia. ; four-stage positive adjustment.

GEARBOX 4-speed with helical gears ; 4th, 3rd, and 2nd, constant mesh with synchromesh engagement ; manual control through light tubes and universal joints from lever mounted centrally in driver's compartment. Ratios : Top, direct ; 3rd, 1·59 to 1 ; 2nd, 2·63 to 1 ; 1st, 5 to 1 ; reverse, 6·13 to 1.

PROPELLOR SHAFTS Open tubular type with 1600 type Hardy Spicer joints with needle roller bearings.

FRONT AXLE "H"-section beam ; stub axles in phosphor bronze bushes ; King pin thrust on hardened steel button ; hubs on taper-roller bearings.

REAR AXLE Full-floating type, cast-steel centre with tubular ends. Single reduction by bevel, giving ratio of 4·625 to 1. Alternative ratios : 4·11 or 5·14 to 1.

STEERING GEAR "Marles" cam-and-double roller, located right or left-hand ; 21 in. steering wheel.

BRAKES Internal expanding ; drum dia., $16\frac{3}{4}$ in. (425 mm.) lining thickness $\frac{1}{2}$ in. (12 mm.) ; lining width, front 4 in. rear 6 in. ; Braking area, foot 577 sq. in. (3723 sq. cm.), hand 346 sq. in. (2210 sq. cm.).

    Foot :—Air-pressure system with operating cylinders on axles. Westinghouse 10 cu. ft. compressor (Export Models). Vacuum-Servo (British Models).

    Hand :—Pull-on type acting on rear wheels.

SPRINGS Semi-elliptic ; 4 in. wide ; front 60 in. (1·524 m.) long ; rear 62 in. (1·584 m.) long.

ELECTRICAL EQUIPMENT 24-volt lighting and starting with insulated return system, including 148 amp. hr. batteries, dynamo, starter, head and side lamps, horn, switchboard, instrument panel, control panel, windscreen wiper and de-froster.

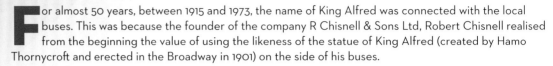

A SHORT HISTORY OF
KING ALFRED MOTOR SERVICES

For almost 50 years, between 1915 and 1973, the name of King Alfred was connected with the local buses. This was because the founder of the company R Chisnell & Sons Ltd, Robert Chisnell realised from the beginning the value of using the likeness of the statue of King Alfred (created by Hamo Thornycroft and erected in the Broadway in 1901) on the side of his buses.

Mr Chisnell Senior started his transport business during the First World War and having gained experience moving troops to and from the local camps, in 1922 started building up a network of local bus services. By 1930 he had established King Alfred as the principal local bus company. It was by no means the only bus operator in the city; there were many smaller independents as well as buses from the mighty area operators of Hants & Dorset, Wilts & Dorset and Aldershot & District.

The routes radiated out from King Alfred's statue in the Broadway to reach Fisher's Pond, Oliver's Battery, Sparsholt, Stockbridge, Crawley, Sutton Scotney, Whitchurch, Overton and Basingstoke, as well as Hookpit to the north east of the city. The fleet consisted of single-deckers until wartime loads brought the first double-decker, an 'unfrozen' Leyland Titan TD7 in 1942.

The Governor, as the founder was called, died in 1945 but his two sons, Fred and Bob, had been brought up in the business. After the war, under their control, King Alfred became the principal local Winchester bus operator with a network of frequent services and a very modern fleet, well-presented in their green and cream colours with that famous likeness of King Alfred on their sides.

Small wonder, then, that they were tempted to buy the ultra-modern Leyland Olympic. Indeed, they went on to continue investing imaginatively in the fleet right up to 1971, when they took delivery of three Metro-Scanias in another revolutionary step! Sad to say, in 1973, with the next generation of Chisnells at retirement age and the current running against private enterprise local buses, the company ceased operations. The buses and routes were taken over by Hants & Dorset.

Throughout their 50 years of operation, the King Alfred buses came and went through the city streets, starting and finishing their journeys by turning in the Broadway under the watchful eye of King Alfred himself.

Today, thanks to the efforts of the Friends of King Alfred buses, that scene can be replicated each New Year's Day, when the preserved buses from the erstwhile fleet of King Alfred come out to operate over their old routes, evoking the memory of a proud local business.

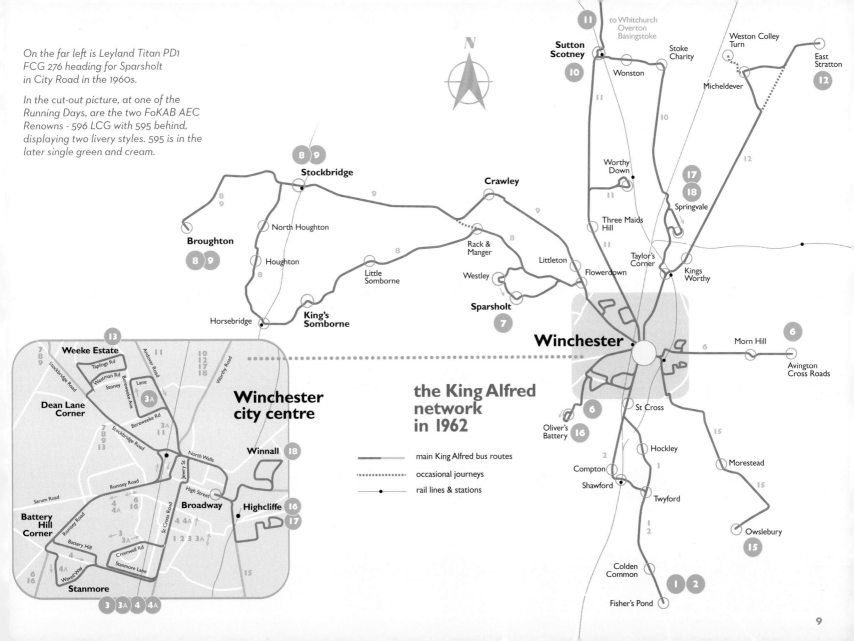

On the far left is Leyland Titan PD1 FCG 276 heading for Sparsholt in City Road in the 1960s.

In the cut-out picture, at one of the Running Days, are the two FoKAB AEC Renowns - 596 LCG with 595 behind, displaying two livery styles. 595 is in the later single green and cream.

JAA 708
IN SERVICE

On the left is JAA 708 standing in Chesil Street outside the King Alfred Hillside bus garage before that was rebuilt in the 1960s to enlarge the entrance.

You can see an intriguing advert for The Fish Shop on the side of the bus.

By 1950, R.Chisnell & Sons Ltd had amassed a fine fleet of post-war Leylands, both double-deck Titans and single-deck Tigers (buses and coaches). Mr Bob Chisnell was always interested in new things, and when the revolutionary Olympic came on the market he was a likely customer. It must have intrigued him to think that by buying an Olympic, King Alfred would have the very first underfloor-engined bus in Winchester – indeed probably in Hampshire! It can be imagined that Leyland worked quite hard to interest Chisnell's in the new bus, which was obviously an off-the-peg product in so many ways. Be that as it may, the new bus was delivered in October 1950 and one of the first things that had to be done was the digging of a new pit in the Hillside garage so that the bus could be properly maintained!

JAA 708 was used on very specific routes, mainly the 4 to Battery Hill and Stanmore and to a lesser extent on the 7 to Sparsholt, as well as on various school services. It was also used on excursions and private hires, where its big 0.600 9.6-litre engine and consequent power and speed made it a popular vehicle. It was evidently less popular on town work, where it had a reputation amongst the drivers for a heavy clutch, though it was also renowned for its speed and ease of climbing the hill of Romsey Road. It settled down on the 4 and for many years was the main vehicle on this route, which ran every half an hour seven days a week until the Sunday service was withdrawn late in 1963.

Most King Alfred buses were sold for scrap, nearly all making their way to the yard of Morgan's in Waltham Chase. JAA 708 was to prove the exception. The reason was tied up with a tragic accident to another bus.

In this picture well-loaded King Alfred JAA 708
is setting off from the Broadway for yet another round trip to Stanmore.
It is passing the aptly-named King Alfred Snack Bar under the watchful gaze
of King Alfred himself - the statue is just out of frame to the left. Do you think the snack bar
ever burnt any cakes?

Behind is one of King Alfred's AEC Bridgemasters, WCG 107, soon to leave on route 13 to Weeke Estate.

Very few photos seem to have been taken of the Olympic in service with King Alfred other than in the Broadway.

However, Robert Jowitt took this beautiful composition of JAA 708 heading for the Broadway along St Cross Road in May 1960.

Here, in an evocative photograph by Fred York, JAA 708 rolls down North Walls approaching its terminus.

The Hants & Dorset Bristol Lodekka LD following it has come all the way from Fareham.

SOUTHERN
ELECTRICITY
BOARD
WINCHESTER BRANCH OFFICE

BROADWAY 4

JAA 708

J 1919
"KING ALFRED"
MOTOR SERVICES
Weekly Ticket
NOT TRANSFERABLE

OUT		IN
MON.		MON.
TUES	Fare......	TUES
WED.	Expiring......between	WED.
THUR	and	FRI.
FRI.	Name......	SAT.
SAT.	Address......

The two colour pictures on this page show JAA 708 in Jimmy Glynn's colours and re-registered BIC 671. The view below, taken by Ken Jubb in September 1968, shows it before it was in use as a school bus, whereas the nearside view on the right appears to have been taken after it was withdrawn in 1977.

The inset black and white picture by Fred York is of the Bedford VAM obtained in part-exchange for the Olympic.

On the opposite page you can see the Olympic outside the St John's Rooms in the Broadway, the starting point of route 4.

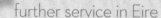

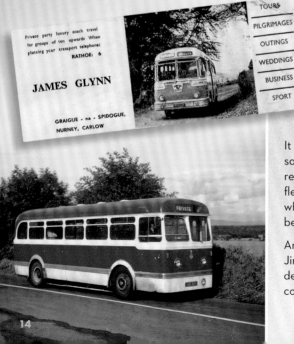

Private party luxury coach travel for groups of ten upwards When planning your transport telephone:
RATHOE: 6

JAMES GLYNN

GRAIGUE - na - SPIDOGUE,
NURNEY, CARLOW

TOURS
PILGRIMAGES
OUTINGS
WEDDINGS
BUSINESS
SPORT

JAA 708 was withdrawn in September 1965, but was not sold for scrap, unlike most King Alfred buses. The story is complex but worth telling. In the same year, Leyland Tiger Cub MAA 4 was involved in a fatal collision on the A33 while working route 12 to East Stratton, as a result of which it was written off. The Chisnells decided to replace it with a cheap Strachans bodied Bedford VAM 46-seater bus, which arrived in March 1966 as EOR 415D, bought through the Farnham dealer, Baker West. In April 1966 JAA 708 went to Baker West and in September a second Bedford VAM, GHO 416D, was delivered to Winchester in part-exchange for the Olympic.

further service in Eire

It was from Baker West that it came to be sold for further service in Ireland. It turned up, resplendent in new red and cream colours, in the fleet of Jimmy Glynn of Graigue-na-Spidogue, where it ran for some years, but seems to have been out of use by August 1976.

And there it lay, parked in *the Showroom* as Jimmy Glynn called the rough field opposite his depot, alongside many other British buses and coaches, awaiting an uncertain fate . . .

14

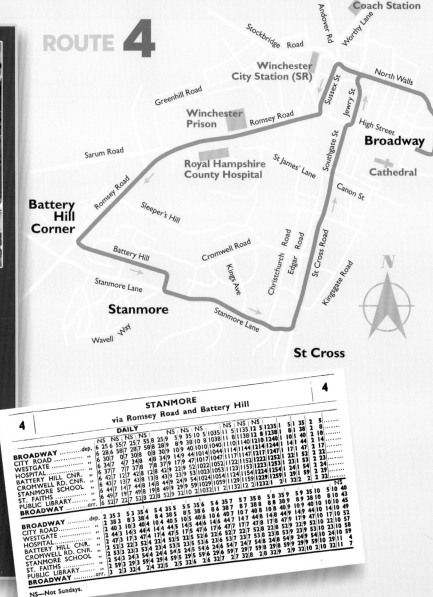

ROUTE 4

Route 4 (service numbers were introduced in 1949) was one of Mr Chisnell's first King Alfred bus routes starting on 9 October 1922. In those early days it proceeded from the Broadway straight up the High Street, through the Westgate and then followed the later route all the way back round to the Broadway. Initially, it ran every two hours, then in 1923 it increased to hourly and by wartime it was almost half-hourly – a frequency to which it settled down from 1949, leaving the Broadway at 05 and 35 minutes past the hour, though early on it was diverted via North Walls, City Road and Sussex Street.

It existed to serve the then new council estates being built at Battery Hill and Stanmore – red brick houses laid out in more-or-less garden village style which developed these parts of Winchester between the wars and were extended westwards after the Second World War.

It ran every day (although it started later on Sundays) and buses operated until after 10 pm. Only in December 1963 did the need for economy force the withdrawal of evening and Sunday services. In 1970, to cope with a severe staff shortage, it was reduced to hourly (at 35 past the hour) and on Mondays to Fridays in early 1973 it had dwindled to three trips a day in the morning off-peak!

STANMORE — via Romsey Road and Battery Hill

NS—Not Sundays.

WE HAVE A PLAN

Friends of King Alfred Buses chairman and founder James Freeman reported the arrival of the bus from Ireland in the February 1991 edition of Buses magazine. This chapter is based on that report.

His forecast for the cost and timescale was perhaps a little optimistic . . .

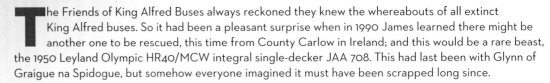

The Friends of King Alfred Buses always reckoned they knew the whereabouts of all extinct King Alfred buses. So it had been a pleasant surprise when in 1990 James learned there might be another one to be rescued, this time from County Carlow in Ireland; and this would be a rare beast, the 1950 Leyland Olympic HR40/MCW integral single-decker JAA 708. This had last been with Glynn of Graigue na Spidogue, but somehow everyone imagined it must have been scrapped long since.

So it was with great excitement and no little trepidation that four members of FoKAB set off to Ireland in April 1990. FoKAB had a friendly agent in Ireland, Tony Leadbetter, who organised the negotiations with the owner Mr Jimmy Glynn. Tony arranged for the team to visit Graigue-na-Spidogue and view that field of rusty buses and coaches the Glynns called *the Showroom*. There, deep in the bushes, but still relatively complete, was BIC 671, alias 708. A happy day was spent digging it out and feeling it all over and, after some tricky negotiations, a deal was struck.

Operation 708 started on 19 June 1990. The Glynns towed 708 to Rosslare where it was pulled on to the ferry to stand next to a gleaming modern coach - to the total amazement of the American tourists just getting off it! On arrival at Fishguard disaster nearly struck when the shunter towing the bus off the ferry by one of the brake pipes changed gear and the pipe broke. But eventually 708 was secured on the back of David Hoare's trusty articulated low loader for the long run back to Winchester. After the most cursory of checks by HM Customs, the journey to Winchester was relatively uneventful and 708 was soon back among friends alongside the other ex-King Alfred buses in the collection.

Soon afterwards the work of rebuilding the bus began and FoKAB set up a restoration fund to raise £15,000 to undertake the necessary work with the aim of JAA 708 being the star attraction at the 1 January 1992 Running Day in Winchester.

Before the Second World War, buses and coaches in the King Alfred fleet were always referred to by a name consisting of their type and a number, thus 'Dennis 6' or 'Victor 2'.

From 1945 on this system started to fall out of use and was replaced by referring to the vehicles by the numbers on their registration plates. At first, these were just whatever was allocated by the Hampshire County Council licensing office, but all this changed after 1949 when John Sincock, latterly Traffic Manager, joined the company. When a new bus or coach was delivered, John would go the licensing office and negotiate for the numbers that would suit the creation of little batches of numbers. Thus, JAA 708 was joined by JAA 705-7 (all Leyland Titans) and much later by CCG 704C (a Bedford VAL coach), EOU 703D (another VAL), JHO 702E (a Bedford VAM) and BCG 701J (a Bedford YRQ coach and the last vehicle delivered to King Alfred). In this way, duplication was avoided and numbers were kept, more or less, together.

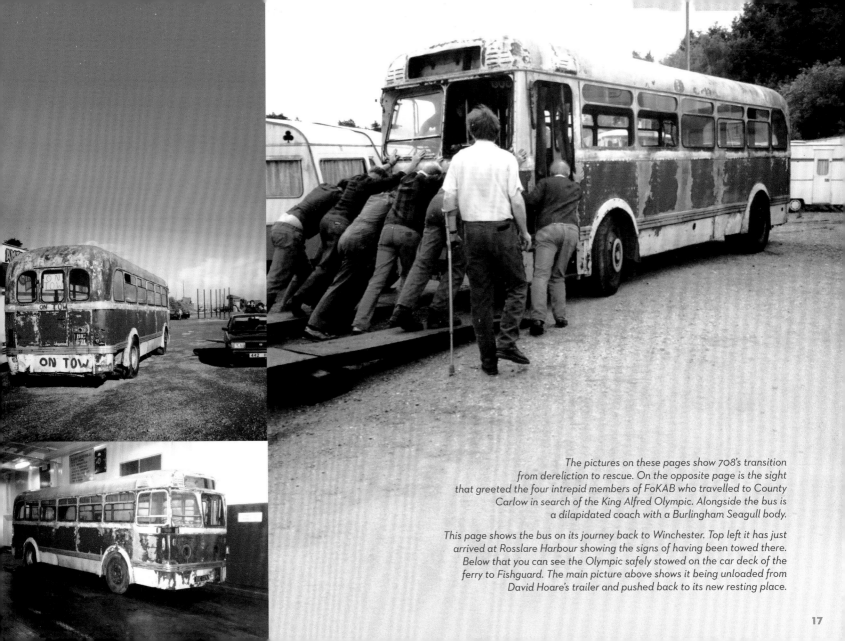

The pictures on these pages show 708's transition from dereliction to rescue. On the opposite page is the sight that greeted the four intrepid members of FoKAB who travelled to County Carlow in search of the King Alfred Olympic. Alongside the bus is a dilapidated coach with a Burlingham Seagull body.

This page shows the bus on its journey back to Winchester. Top left it has just arrived at Rosslare Harbour showing the signs of having been towed there. Below that you can see the Olympic safely stowed on the car deck of the ferry to Fishguard. The main picture above shows it being unloaded from David Hoare's trailer and pushed back to its new resting place.

THE WILDERNESS YEARS

As JAA 708 was being brought back to Hampshire, FoKAB members had visions of its early restoration and return to pristine condition.

In fact, this ambition was to take 22 years to fulfil, but at least the Olympic's future was assured as it stood quietly at FoKAB's Chandler's Ford base.

In the excitement of bringing 708 back to Winchester, nobody in FoKAB would have believed that it would take another 22 years to complete the project and put this historic bus back on the road.

FoKAB has only ever had limited resources at its disposal and the energy of its volunteers can only really be aimed at one major project at a time.

Not long after the Olympic arrived at the group's headquarters, some 10 miles from Winchester, came the news that the 1956 Leyland Titan PD2 PoU 494 was available in Augusta, Georgia, to repatriate to Winchester.

The work to get 494 back started in earnest in 1992. FoKAB bought a partly-restored former Leicester 1962 Park Royal bodied Leyland Titan PD3 double decker, TBC 162. The purpose was to complete this in King Alfred livery so that it could be taken to Augusta and exchanged for 494. The latter itself arrived in Winchester in the autumn of 1993, but took five years to complete – it was relaunched in 1998.

On the way home: Pete Staples' picture on the immediate left is of David Hoare's trusty Atkinson heading south through Newbury on the A34.

On the far left, and not long afterwards, 708 makes its triumphant arrival at FoKAB's base.

Above is the bus in the space that, in the event, it was to occupy for almost 12 years.

Just in view is the 1959 Leyland Tiger Cub WCG 104 which was the first bus in the FoKAB collection and was here undergoing renovation.

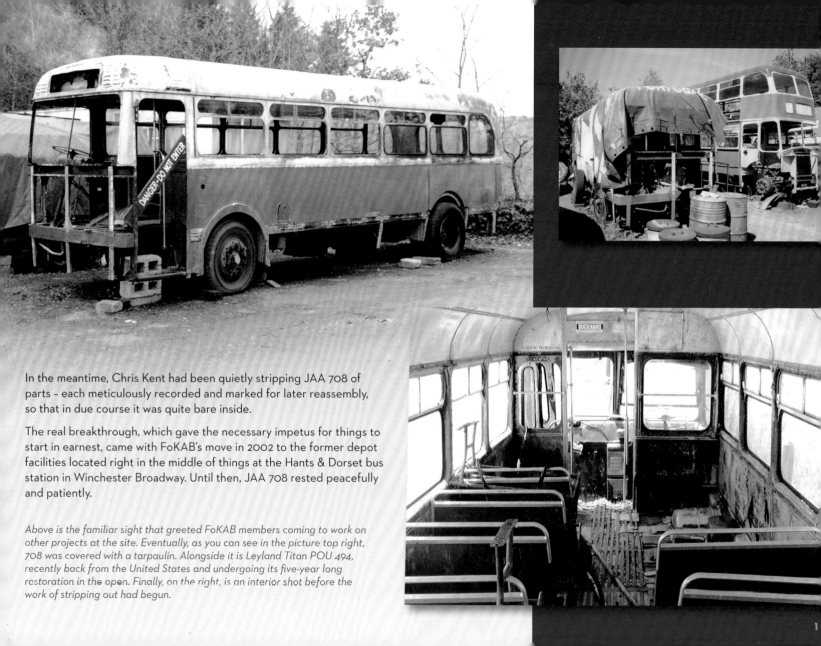

In the meantime, Chris Kent had been quietly stripping JAA 708 of parts – each meticulously recorded and marked for later reassembly, so that in due course it was quite bare inside.

The real breakthrough, which gave the necessary impetus for things to start in earnest, came with FoKAB's move in 2002 to the former depot facilities located right in the middle of things at the Hants & Dorset bus station in Winchester Broadway. Until then, JAA 708 rested peacefully and patiently.

Above is the familiar sight that greeted FoKAB members coming to work on other projects at the site. Eventually, as you can see in the picture top right, 708 was covered with a tarpaulin. Alongside it is Leyland Titan POU 494, recently back from the United States and undergoing its five-year long restoration in the open. Finally, on the right, is an interior shot before the work of stripping out had begun.

THE RESTORATION

Stephen Morris kept readers of Bus & Coach Preservation magazine up to date with the progress of the restoration of JAA 708 in an occasional series of articles over a decade. It was a mammoth task, as you will discover.

What follows is closely based on those articles. Dates for each section refer to the issue of Bus & Coach Preservation in which the original article appeared.

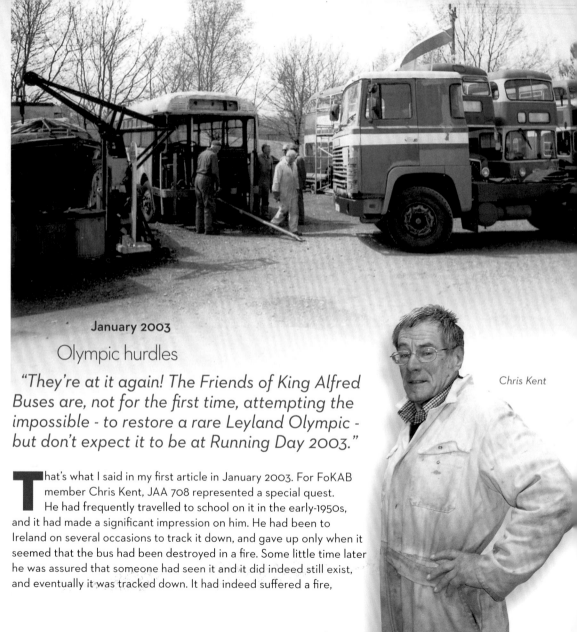

January 2003

Olympic hurdles

"They're at it again! The Friends of King Alfred Buses are, not for the first time, attempting the impossible - to restore a rare Leyland Olympic - but don't expect it to be at Running Day 2003."

Chris Kent

That's what I said in my first article in January 2003. For FoKAB member Chris Kent, JAA 708 represented a special quest. He had frequently travelled to school on it in the early-1950s, and it had made a significant impression on him. He had been to Ireland on several occasions to track it down, and gave up only when it seemed that the bus had been destroyed in a fire. Some little time later he was assured that someone had seen it and it did indeed still exist, and eventually it was tracked down. It had indeed suffered a fire, but only a very minor one and was still complete! Negotiations were put in place with the owner - who, it seems, was not actually very keen on negotiating - and the bus changed hands for rather a lot of punts in 1990. As mentioned earlier, a posse of FoKAB members made their way to Rosslare on the ferry from Fishguard to meet the bus, and were rather worried when it got to about 10 minutes from departure time and there was still no bus. However a pair of headlights were spotted, and a Ford Transit rolled up with an Olympic in tow, the little van having hauled it about 60 miles!

getting started

Once FoKAB had access to its undercover workshop the Olympic was moved into the new premises in 2002 and work began in earnest. With MCW's advanced construction techniques it was thought that the job of restoring it should not be hugely difficult, but would be lengthy.

Though badly corroded there were enough pieces of waistrail and other sections intact to enable new pieces to be fabricated, which was done some time ago, and it was to be a question of replacing one bay at a time. There is no complex woodwork in the main structure at all. Panelling is aluminium, and the original panels have survived remarkably well; these are for the most part reuseable, though when the time came to reassemble the bus FoKAB had to apply a barrier between the steel structure and aluminium panels to prevent electrolytic corrosion taking place.

FoKAB is very fortunate with the level of cooperation it has received from Stagecoach South, and one of its bodybuilding staff went through the bus to suggest a programme of works for it. The first job was to make sure the structure was straight. The wheels were removed and the vehicle jacked up to ensure it was square, standing on blocks. The floor and side lining panels were taken out to inspect the state of the structure underneath, and the next job would be to remove the ceiling panels to inspect the roof structure. The underframe was is in good condition too, with little more than surface rust. Though the idea of integral construction was to have a comparatively lightweight structure, in fact the Olympic's is a very solid affair with two enormous longitudinal members, just like the side members on a conventional chassis, and these have withstood years of standing in a field remarkably well, just needing to be cleaned up and coated in red oxide. The body framing, lighter in section, had not fared so well, however, and was badly corroded, especially around the front end where the door was left open.

The bus was largely complete when it came back from Ireland, but once the front panels were removed what was left underneath them was in a very parlous state. New glass-fibre mouldings were made for the windscreen surrounds, intended to replace the metal originals. More serious was water ingress into the bottom rail which was very badly corroded. The plan was to replace the framework at the front and rear corners, which were by far the worst bits, and then work towards the centre from either end, hoping each part of the old frame would be removed without too much difficulty and a new replacement piece riveted into its place.

The main picture opposite shows Malcolm Millard (he's the one on the left) about to hook up 708 to his Scania truck in preparation for its departure to Winchester.

On the far left 708 is safely stored indoors in FoKAB's Central Works, courtesy of Stagecoach.

Above, the work begins in earnest. All the interior up to the window frames has been stripped away, exposing the heavy underframe and some of the framework of the integral construction.

The only answer to the dilapidated entrance area of the bus was almost complete reconstruction, as is all too evident in the picture above.

Keith Morton is on the right - mission impossible?

On the opposite page you can see that calling the bus a rust-coloured skeleton was no exaggeration.

The steps also needed replacing; these had been driven into the ground and completely rotted away. Luckily, virtually all other parts were there and many were removed from the bus and retained; in particularly good condition were the stainless steel wheelarches which looked almost new, and there was a full set of the Olympic's distinctive beading. Missing were three seats, while three of the distinctive offside sliding vents had been replaced by some more commonplace ones, and sourcing replacements looked as if it would be a problem. The mechanical units were in good condition - the engine started, and ran, after only 15sec of turning over, and comparatively little attention was going to be needed.

The plan was to remove the ceiling panels, then the next job would be to take out all the running units so they could be worked on separately from the bus itself and reinstalled at a later stage. FoKAB's preservation coordinator Keith Morton, who was masterminding the job, described it as, *"mission impossible, restoration impossible!"*

"We'd been led to believe it was OK, but when we saw it it was covered in moss and kids had been running around on the roof," he said.

It may have then looked like mission impossible, but hopefully restoration would indeed be possible - but had it used the conventional composite construction of the day it seems quite likely that there would have been nothing to restore. I reported then: *"As it is, it will be a slow and tedious job but hopefully one which will not involve massive levels of skill. Look out for it at Running Day 2008!"*

May 2005

The Olympic had got to a significant stage now, in that it was about to be moved out of FoKAB's workshops for the next phase of its restoration.

Bus restoration often involves taking one step forward and several steps back, and looking at JAA 708 then, more than two years on, that certainly was the case. When we saw it before, the Olympic had no wheels and no floor, but it looked something like a bus. It had been propped up on blocks to straighten

under its own weight, and looking at it now it seemed pretty straight. What there was of it, that is! In the ensuing months virtually all the panels were removed from it and stored away. Made of an aircraft-grade aluminium, called Duralumin, they were in superb condition and would go back on the bus later. Indeed most of the visible bits of bus were in excellent condition, such as wheelarches and window pans. But all those were currently off the bus and beneath the skin it was in a bit of a sorry state.

We had previously suggested that the ceiling panels were also to be removed, but they and the roof panels were still in place. It had been decided to leave well alone, and the roof looked as straight as a die, suggesting that there was probably nothing seriously amiss under the skin. The upright members were also in pretty good condition; like many more modern buses the uprights are actually continuous hoops creating the main structure of the body. FoKAB was well aware though that the longitudinal members at floor and waist level were shot, and the remaining metal had become very thin and corroded, in places with serious holes in them.

Replacing them was going to be a lengthy process; whereas the uprights are continuous members, the side members are short lengths joining the uprights by diamond-shaped flitch plates.

Without its panels and window pans the Olympic now resembled a rust-coloured skeleton, but it showed exactly what work needed to be done. The very heavy underframe had a coating of surface rust but was as solid as the day it was built. All the mechanical units were in place, and while the engine wouldn't win any beauty contests then, it had recently been run and checked by an engineer that knows his Leylands. His diagnosis was that it was in extremely fine fettle and FoKAB were advised not to touch it.

FoKAB have, down the years, proved themselves to be a very capable organisation with an amazing commitment to conserving their own piece of Hampshire's history, and this was recognised by Hampshire County Council's Museum Service, which awarded the Olympic grant aid on a match-funding basis. This enabled FoKAB to have the Olympic taken away to be shot blasted intact, complete with running units in place, then coated and silvered.

Those longitudinal members may have been enough to make lesser men weep, but FoKAB was aware of the problem it was up against from the beginning. What did exist was used as patterns to make up new ones soon after it came back from Ireland. These two phases were expected to take somewhere in the region of six months or so - not that it's ever safe to predict these things! - and would be a major step forward for the Olympic. With the original panels and most of the window pans ready to go straight back on to it, I understood that progress should then be very much swifter than it had been so far - much to the relief of Chris Kent, whose particular baby the Olympic was; he couldn't quite believe how many years had elapsed since that great day when the Olympic returned to its native soil.

Job done! Ian Meader and Peter Carter stand proudly showing off the shot-blasted and reconstructed framework outside their premises at Romsey.

A few weeks earlier you can see the bus in Ian's workshop with Eric Chambers measuring the entrance in early preparations for reconstructing that area.

Eric was a body maker at Park Royal Vehicles before setting up LPC Coachworks at Hounslow, which famously undertook a number of restoration challenges for the late Prince Marshall.

December 2005

When I last looked at JAA 708 it was just about to go off and have its chassis shot-blasted. That happened, the chassis was silvered and it then looked set to support the bus for another half century or so.

The grant funding from Hampshire Museums Service, on a match-funding basis, meant the fortunes of this rather sickly bus had been transformed. Sickly structurally, that is, though apparently when it returned from Ireland they connected up some batteries and fuel under gravity feed, and after only 15sec or so churning on the starter it blew out clouds of smoke and assorted gunge before settling down to an even tickover. The horizontal Leyland

O.600 engine was deemed to be in excellent condition and was left alone in the time-honoured philosophy of 'if it ain't broke, don't fix it'.

The new set of longitudinal members for the body, fabricated when the Olympic came back from Ireland, were now fitted. The job was put outside, to Ian Meader's IM Services, a specialist commercial vehicle repairer with a love for old vehicles. It's based near Romsey, and tackles almost any bodywork job on a commercial vehicle. It hadn't then done many buses, though an RML-type Routemaster had recently been painted in its 16ft high by 45ft long paint booth.

I'd suggested in the previous report that fitting the framing back together would be a simple if laborious task. Laborious it was, simple: well, maybe not. They found that the longitudinal sections were a fraction short, but with flitch plates to bolt them on to the uprights, this was not a great problem. More of a problem were the diagonal members made up by IM Services from steel channel. This should have been a straightforward job, but even the eagle-eyed Chris Kent and Keith Morton who were masterminding the project,

Here is the newly-reconstructed integral frame ready to be transported back to Winchester.

and both with a very keen eye for detail, had overlooked the fact that as the panels are slightly curved towards the bottom rail, the diagonals are not quite straight. Indeed they are gently curved in two planes, and IM have developed a technique using two halves of a railway sleeper to bend the channel to just the right shape. One of the original members served as a pattern, but they found that fitting the frame together was very much a question of trial and error, involving several attempts to get each part to fit.

However the bottom rail on the offside was now in place between the wheelarches, and the waistrail well on the way. Already JAA 708 is much the sturdier for it, even though the nearside still had more little perforations than a certain make of teabag, and some not so little either.

Though of integral construction, the Olympic still boasts a massive chassis, and this was largely solid, though some additional material had to be let into one side member near the front axle, and the same was needed towards the rear of the bus. At the same time Bob Smith took off the front brakes to refurbish.

The roof remained in place; there seemed little need to disturb it, although there were large dents in the rear dome which would need to be dealt with and there was some discussion whether that should be tackled by removing it from the bus or pushing it out from inside, either of which would unfortunately involve disturbing the roof structure.

Ruth Andrews - third from left - had come forward to lead the project and would see it right through to completion.

She is accompanied here - from left to right - by Melvyn Lovelock, husband Keith Andrews, in the bus Pete Staples, Sylvia Muspratt, Keith Morton and Barry Thomas.

Sylvia was a King Alfred employee from the late 1950s until its demise in 1973 and, like other former King Alfred staff, has taken a keen interest in the Olympic project.

As mentioned previously, the panelwork of the bus was all in very good order. Although the Olympic looked as if it still had a very long way to go, in fact once the framework was completed a major corner would have been turned and a start made again in turning it back into something resembling a bus.

September 2007

an Olympic for the Olympics?

At this point in September 2007 I recorded that there was still a long time to go, but the Friends were feeling confident the Olympic would be ready for The Olympics (the 2012 ones), though they would actually like to see it finished in time for its 60th birthday in October 2010.

Back in 2005 JAA 708 was at IM Services, where the steel longitudinal and diagonal sections of the body construction were being slotted back into place in a painstaking process. That work had now been completed, with the exception of one diagonal which needed to go in on the rearmost nearside bay to support the fuel filler.

As a result JAA was looking a bit more complete, though still lacking most of its panels, and was at least very solid. The only real worry was over the lower end of some of the aluminium verticals which had become bent over the years and might not bend back very easily. It returned to FoKAB's Central Works from IM Services on a low loader in March 2007.

There was also a new project leader, Ruth Andrews, who may well be familiar to visitors to FoKAB's sales stand, which she and her husband Keith run. Ruth admits it had been a steep learning curve and she had to learn the names of all the different bits of the bus, though the way items like the steering idler trip off her tongue you would think she had been brought up in Leyland's Farington works, but for the lack of a strong Lancastrian accent. Indeed she had to explain that very component to me; it's bolted to the front axle (well it wasn't at the time, but you get my meaning) and everything else in the steering gear effectively revolves around it. The pin in the middle of it that makes all this happen was worn and away for refurbishing.

On the bus's return to Central Works, Ruth and Keith Andrews got on with painting the framework with red primer and dark blue paint, and after some deliberation, the chassis, which had been silvered before it went to IM Services, now had a coat of chassis black.

mechanical progress

Various mechanical components were currently off the vehicle; most noticeable was the front axle with various items needing attention. There was a bit of a problem obtaining rubber seals for the brake diaphragms. The chambers themselves were scored, though not too badly. It was hoped that once the rubber seals had been tracked down, they might overcome the problem, but if not they'd need some metal spraying. A new kingpin repair kit was sourced for the nearside, and the front springs were off for attention. One had a split in the second leaf down and the other a patch in the top leaf. As was often the case, the nearside one has an extra leaf to counteract the effect of the road camber.

We've already noted that the otherwise solid chassis had needed some metal letting into it near the nearside front axle. This led to a great deal of head-scratching about a sizeable casting which locates the front shock absorber. No-one could work out quite where it went; screw holes in its top face lined up with holes in the top flange of the chassis, but screw holes in the back face of the piece had no corresponding holes in the side member. The patching was then remembered, and whenever it had been done someone

By 2007 the Olypic restoration was advancing apace. Note the original entrance doors standing over to the left.

forgot it needed bolt holes for the shock absorber mounting. Like most Leyland single-deckers, the Olympic only had shock absorbers on the front; rear shock absorbers didn't become standard until single-deckers reached 12m long, which explains why the ride at the back of a 36ft Leopard can be very lively. Hopefully at only 27ft long and with a relatively short rear overhang the Olympic won't be quite so bouncy.

Away from the front axle, the radiator and fuel tank were refurbished by Kingston Radiators in Southampton; the fuel pump and injectors had also been overhauled and returned and the dynamo was away in Hedge End being overhauled. A new engine air intake had also been obtained, though at this point without any gauze.

It had been hoped to leave the main mechanical units in situ, but sand penetrated the clutch and gearbox when the frame was sandblasted and they had to be removed for cleaning out.

FoKAB's 'chief mug'

Meanwhile another of FoKAB's volunteers, Barry Thomas, found himself rewiring the bus. Describing himself as 'chief mug,' Barry trained as an engineer with a munitions firm but since turned his hand to all manner of things. He'd never rewired a bus before, but he had rewired buildings and motorhomes.

There was much debate during the restoration about whether JAA's crowning glory should be disturbed or not; I remember the first time I saw JAA, not long after it came back from Ireland, FoKAB president, the irrepressibly optimistic James Freeman, not being too bothered about the bus's many near-impossible challenges, because the ceiling panels were in such good order. The roof was less healthy, as kids loved jumping on it when it was laid up in Ireland, and the best way to sort the roof would be to push it back into shape from inside: which meant disturbing those wonderful ceiling panels. The roof is all aluminium and pop-riveted in place, so taking it off would be very difficult. Not that the ceiling panels are easy to remove either, but Barry was working on taking them off to get at the wiring. Already the rear ones had been taken out, and the major dents in the rear dome pushed out to good effect.

Their removal also revealed wooden packing pieces for the light fittings, and those in the rear dome are quite exquisitely shaped to accommodate the complex curves of the roof dome. They were also completely rotten and would need some very skilled carpentry to replace. The good news was, they were one of the very few wooden components on this carefully-engineered all-metal bus.

They realised light fittings would be a problem. There are 12 of them - or rather there weren't, which was the problem. There were however 10 back plates; making up the two missing ones was going to be less of a problem than making up 12 of the rather decorative light fittings.

Barry started a complete rewire, using modern materials. Some major electrical components proved reasonably easy to source - eBay yielded a few - but some CAV items in particular were difficult to find.

other bits & pieces

Another FoKAB volunteer, Melvyn Lovelock, who has been involved in the project right through, was stripping paint from the rear emergency door when the remains of an advert for Westcombe Motors of City Road Winchester, evident on pictures of the bus nearly 50 years ago, came to light. Such evidence of the bus's authenticity would have been helpful when FoKAB was wrestling with the problem of getting its original registration number back, which it did succeed in doing.

Talking of registration numbers, JAA 708 already had some splendid new number plates ready to go on the bus, though fitting them had not yet become quite a priority! FoKAB had been in the habit of showing a display board about JAA at events, and it was seen by someone from classic number plate manufacturer Framptons at Waterlooville, who volunteered a pair of plates for the bus. Expecting them to be pressed aluminium, Framptons were as good as their word, even when it transpired the plates on the bus were painted and they had to go out and hire a signwriter to produce them.

Opposite top left is FoKAB's 'chief mug' Barry Thomas, here grinding a brake drum.

Below that is the ceiling removed, revealing the wooden packing pieces for the light fittings. All these had to be replaced.

Above is Melvyn Lovelock exposing the advert for Westcombe Motors that used to adorn the bus in its heyday, as you can see inside the back cover of this book. This was proof positive that the bus really was JAA 708.

Above is the bus being pushed out of Central Works for display at the 2009 Running Day. To the right the Mayor of Winchester does his bit to help FoKAB raise funds for the project.

Below is part of the rebuilt suspension with a new shock absorber bought off-the-shelf.

Further down the line three seat frames were missing, while further major expense would be incurred in reupholstering all the seats - the cushion filling had crumbled away to powder - and replacing the tyres. Grant funding from Hampshire County Council helped, as had the fact that IM Services charged a very reasonable £8,000 for the considerable job of putting all the framework together and associated tasks.

January 2009

Olympic progress

JAA 708 put in an appearance at the 2009 New Year's Day running day, but didn't have any seats and only went just outside the doors of FoKAB's Central Works! It looked bus-shaped and was sitting happily on its own wheels, some now fetchingly painted green as a sign of things to come.

That its appearance on 1 January was even a possibility represented real progress. It had been one of those periods when much of the work had gone on beneath the surface. Indeed, the fuel pump had been overhauled and the engine run: but other mechanical components hadn't been touched yet, so it had to be pushed into position. But the fact that this was now a rolling shell showed it had moved on a stage.

axle progress

Back in 2007 JAA 708 had been lacking a front axle. Not only was that back on, but the bus was now sitting on its own wheels, and looking pretty straight too. There was some concern that the frame might have been slightly out of true from movement without its panels in place, but it looked very square. Proof of the pudding was going to be when the panels went back on.

The front springs had been rebuilt by Jones Springs of Darlaston; they were tempered and at least one leaf replaced. Rear springs were still in good condition. New shackle pins were specially made by Ashley Precision of Poole, sourced through Norman Aish, and polyurethane bushes from Batchelor Polyurethanes of Birmingham were fitted. Original Metalastik bushes would have featured, but these were no longer available. Ashley Precision also made up a new steering idler nut and all the steering gear was now in place and working, with new kingpins made and fitted too.

New telescopic shock absorbers were sourced for the front end; once the part number was found these were virtually off-the-shelf items. Tracing the part numbers was not easy: the old Leyland part numbers did not coincide with anything on the computer, but it was remembered that new shock absorbers were obtained for one of King Alfred's Leyland Tiger Cubs not too long before, and they yielded a Koni part number, which simplified things rather.

The brake chambers were scored internally, but these were hand polished, and Tim Nicholson had ring seals made. All the brake pipes were off the bus but ready to go back on, and the air reservoir had been cleaned up and successfully pressure-tested to 300psi. Chris Kent was working on the dump valve when I was there.

The expensive side of bus restoration reared its head with the fulcrum block for the accelerator and brake pedal. With its air brakes JAA 708 has an organ-pedal type of brake pedal, like the accelerator, and both pivot inside the same block mounted on the front of the underframe. This had worn beyond reuse and a new one had to be cast from scratch; this small, apparently insignificant component will seldom if ever see the light of day once the bus is completed, but is safety-critical and cost around £400.

The handbrake linkage was overhauled; Ruth Andrews had kept one of the clevis pins with which it was presumably still running in service, and this was worn beyond belief: these had, not surprisingly, been replaced with new ones. Evidence of the 'think of a number, double it then add a bit for safety' approach to engineering of the time was clear in the rotating shaft that transfers movement from the handbrake rod to the rear brakes, which looked as if it held the entire bus together. But the handbrake was now all connected up and was looking good. Unusually, the Olympic has its handbrake lever to the left of the steering wheel, right next to the gear lever and there was some concern as to whether the gear lever and the handbrake lever would foul each other. Much of the heavy work, incidentally, such as replacing the springs and shackle pins and the engine stays, refitting the front axle and the handbrake linkage was undertaken by Charlie Lemon.

ceiling the argument

James Freeman, who has since returned to the role of FoKAB's chairman, is well-known as a visionary. It is partly down to his vision that King Alfred buses have been dragged back to Winchester from around the globe.

That vision was brought home to me the first time he proudly showed me his new acquisition from Ireland some 18 years ago. If I'm honest, I was finding it difficult to find much positive to say about the heap of junk on wheels that had been dragged back, apparently involving a lengthy tow behind, not a Matador nor

At the top are the accelerator and brake pedals mounted in the new fulcrum block, while in the cut-out picture you can compare the old worn block with its pristine replacement.

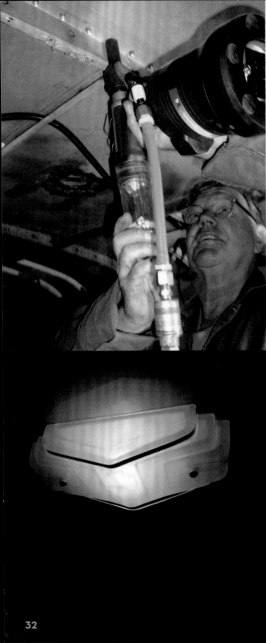

heavy Scammell, but a Transit van, and with nothing more than a handbrake (with, as is now known, very dodgy clevis pins!) to control the bus - before it reached British soil that is. But James seemed to see the holes in the bus and other deficiencies as mere trifles to be sorted out one Sunday afternoon and was ecstatic about the wonderful state of the ceiling. And yes, it was in good condition, it has to be said.

I mention this because those ceiling panels had been the source of some debate. They were nice and it would have been nice to leave them untouched. But inside the ceiling is wiring for the lighting, and if you remember the roof was not quite as nature intended, as it had provided a useful playground for Irish kids, apparently with hobnail boots, so was not quite the same shape as it was when it left Weymann's Addlestone works all those years ago. Removing those hallowed ceiling panels enabled Barry Thomas to wield a rubber hammer at the roof panels in situ, and the roof now looks rather more as it would have done 60 years ago.

In order to ensure the roof stayed the right shape, a few extra suitably-shaped wooden ribs were inserted into the roof structure. Each of the wooden pieces holding the lamp bases in place had gone rotten at its outer end, where moisture tends to gather and Melvyn Lovelock scarfed in new pieces to replace the rotten sections. These were all painted and the missing lamp bases were sourced from Colin Billington via Eric Chambers, who also produced a dozen suitable light fittings. Not identical to the originals, they were a good match, to the style of the period. The same applies to moquette: Tim Stubbs had had a run made up for a Rotherham trolleybus and as always the minimum length of a bespoke run is considerably longer than one needed for one bus, so FoKAB acquired sufficient from him for the Olympic. Again it was not absolutely to the original pattern but considered close enough, even for Chris Kent.

Those ceiling panels were all given two coats of primer, two coats of undercoat and two coats of gloss and refitting started; a new lighting circuit was fitted first, of course. All were relieved when that job was finished, as the panels were not easy to store and completely occupied the committee room.

Despite leaving the roof panels in place, their heavy duty rivets had all either stretched or broken and needed replacing. Winchester City Council, through its Community Chest Scheme, kindly donated £400 towards the cost of an Avdelok rivet gun: an appropriate tool given that Leyland's next serious attempt at an integral single-decker, the Leyland National, was held together almost entirely by Avdelok rivets.

And the first couple of window pans had now been refitted. All the windows were reglazed by a local glass supplier, but the frames for the separate sliding sections were thankfully all in reasonable condition. Indeed there was some despondency when the bus first came back that some were missing: incredibly Philip Kirk found the missing ones in Ireland and rolled up in Winchester with them in the boot of his car.

Already the resurrection of JAA 708 had thrown up some seemingly insurmountable challenges, and the team knew there were more to come. Next on the agenda would be the windscreen surrounds; the frames for the windscreens are aluminium and very solid, but the surrounds themselves were now very fetching filigree and one in particular was more 'gree' than 'filli': half of it didn't exist. Then there was the question of finding some Weymann's 7ft 6in seats, as three were missing. Chris Kent looked longingly at the Silver Star Weymann-bodied Atlantean parked close to the Olympic and conjectured about cutting a couple of inches out of three of its seats, but somehow we suspect they might have been missed.

January 2010

Well, JAA 708 did make it to the annual New Year's Day bash, also known as the King Alfred Running Day in 2009 as predicted. For the following great binary date, 010110, it was hoped it might turn up under its own power.

just when it was going so well

All was looking so good. Having sat immobile in Ireland for more than 15 years, FoKAB people had tried starting the bus after its arrival in England. About 15sec churning on the starter was enough for it to roar into life, and after blanketing everything in the inevitably clag it needed to discharge, it sat down to a sweet, even tickover. Some 18 years later, they tried the same trick.

The fuel tank was away for repairs: Ruth Andrews proudly showed me what looked like a very nice jar of Nescafé Gold Blend and was in fact all the flakes of rust left in the tank last time it was 'overhauled'. So a Jerry can was filled with diesel and connected to the bus.

This time it didn't even need 15sec churning on the starter: as Chris Kent told me, it burst into life as soon as the first piston reached the top of the cylinder. However it didn't settle down like a sewing machine, but hunted in true Leyland fashion, only more so. Adjustment of the idle speed on the governor is not straightforward and it could need specialist attention.

FoKAB had been advised they had a good engine, so leave it alone, and that to some extent is what they did. They had naturally seen to some of the auxiliaries, such as new belts. The air intake was also a puzzle; a restored air filter box was fitted, from a Tiger Cub, and though it fitted it didn't seem at all right. One puzzle was that the actual air intake seemed to come out behind the front wheel, right where every bit of road dirt and dead leaves would be shovelled straight into it;

Above is Graham Green (on the left) working with Chris Kent on the back axle. On the right is the back axle with the differential cover off - you can see the refurbished cover below.

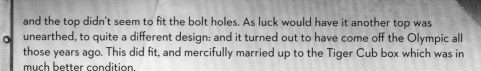

and the top didn't seem to fit the bolt holes. As luck would have it another top was unearthed, to quite a different design: and it turned out to have come off the Olympic all those years ago. This did fit, and mercifully married up to the Tiger Cub box which was in much better condition.

The mystery was solved: on the Olympic, the air is actually drawn from within the saloon through ducting, and not from behind the front wheel at all. This was a sort of early air conditioning system: stale air was drawn out of the saloon by the engine. Quite what the effect all that 1950s cigarette smoke had on performance will probably never be known, with 21st century legislation ensuring that the O.600 engine has probably drawn its last gasp of nicotine.

With the engine running it was time to see what else happened. Fitting new water hoses had disturbed the water pump and some leaks were quickly detected. The air tank, which was off the bus but had been pressure tested last year when we looked at it, was now supplied with new bands and was on the bus, under the cab floor, with its own pressure gauge: not ideally positioned for the driver, when there's enough of a cab to make it driveable, but a pressure gauge nonetheless. This sailed happily up to 82psi, at which point the dump valve did its stuff: all very promising.

With the back axle off, all four gears and reverse were tried and the propshaft rotated in such a way as to show that they all work. Mind you, it also rotated in neutral, which was a bit more worrying, though Chris Kent put that down to the glutinous state of the oil in the gearbox.

differential differences

That back axle, however, was causing a lot of head scratching. Problem one came to light when the back cover was removed from the differential. Various sundry pieces of metal floating around sounded alarm bells. More alarm bells sounded when some were identified as roller bearings; the Olympic back axle should have ball bearings. Disassembly showed roller bearing races around the pinion, one of which was shot to pieces, and some of the unidentified parts turned out to be shards of metal from the disintegrating casing of this race.

Although not a component subject to a lot of stress, the diff cover itself was showing signs of fatigue, possibly emanating from its retaining bolts having been overtightened at some stage, and as two FoKAB members were heading off to the Scottish Vintage Bus Museum at Lathalmond, they took the diff cover with them to see if anything could be done to it. The good doctors of Lathalmond took one look at it and pronounced that it wasn't a bus component at all.

Further alarm bells sounded when it was realised that the halfshafts were longer than they should be for the 7ft 6in bus, which might explain why the rear wheelarches had been horribly botched at some stage. Examination of photographs of the bus in Ireland, compared withhave been.

The good news was, odd bits of metal rattling about where odd bits of metal should not be rattling about did not seem to have affected either the pinion or the crownwheel adversely: both were in good condition, other of course, than one rather damaged bearing on the pinion. It could be that the wrong bearings had been forced in, resulting in one disintegrating.

This is the back axle from the nearside.

Barry Thomas is getting ready to work on the roof.

The mystery of the rear axle thickened. Unlike later axles, where the housing is one big casting, on the Olympic the diff housing and halfshaft tubes are separate pieces, bolted together, and the axle retained these. It was compounded by the fact that the brakes showed signs of being a hybrid of airbrake and vacuum brake components, with both manual and automatic slack adjusters evident, and shoes to the spec you would expect of vacuum brakes, though JAA does have air brakes. This may be less of a mystery than it seems: it was actually built with vacuum brakes, though converted to air very early on.

This heavily-built bus would certainly have struggled with vacuum brakes; Leyland was never brilliant in the brakes department and I well remember driving a late-model Ulsterbus Leyland Tiger brand new from the factory and almost standing on the pedal, white knuckles gripping the steering wheel, wondering if the thing would ever come to a halt! (It did, otherwise I wouldn't be writing this . . .) The Olympic, it seems, was delivered to Winchester on its vacuum brakes, and probably converted by Leyland people before it entered service. So does this multiplicity of parts suggest the job was not done too thoroughly way back then, or is the axle a complete amalgam of Leyland parts cobbled together in later life?

It seemed like a mystery that would never be resolved; it was hoped the problem of sourcing a correct rear axle for a 7ft 6in Olympic might be solved, but with only 21 built, it wouldn't be easy. Don't suggest to FoKAB they get an axle off a 7ft 6in PD2; they listened very politely to my suggestion to that effect before pointing out that the PD2 has an offset diff, which the Olympic doesn't. I wasn't the only person to make that suggestion that day, and they had to explain it patiently again. We also discussed whether a 7ft 6in Tiger Cub axle would do the trick; it seems Leyland didn't build them however. 'What about the Jersey ones?' I ventured, and as I did I conjured up a mental image of such a bus: with the rear wheels right out to the extremities of the wheelarches. Clearly, there wasn't a suitable Tiger Cub axle.

The conundrum now was whether to try restoring the axle on the bus and putting up with it being a tad wide, not too easy until someone worked out what the axle actually was, or hang on and see if an Olympic axle dropped out of the sky. Chris Kent mournfully recalled being about to set out to recover a 7ft 6in Olympic from an Isle of Man scrapyard, only to be told someone had just broken it up; with the benefit of 20:20 hindsight he could have gone over and brought back the rear axle! Dwelling on 'might-have-beens' never does any of us any good.

A 'third way' might have been the more pragmatic solution of using an Eaton axle from a 7ft 6in Bristol LH, which looked as if it could drop in quite simply (famous last words . . .). FoKAB's Barry Thomas bravely, and optimistically, agreed to take on the challenge of finding a solution.

Brake drums and shoes needed replacing: the drums looked great but, at Ruth Andrews' invitation, I ran my hand round the inside of one of them and it could have been made of corrugated iron. Skimming would thus not be an option, and I conjectured what sort of noise they might make if they were put on the bus as was.

Following the engine being run, the exhaust manifold was removed and was found to be in a rough state; some of the flanges where it bolted to the cylinder head were broken, and as their rough edges were caked in soot it would seem it ran in service like that for some time.

So there was a lot to do before the bus would be ready to creep into Winchester bus station under its own steam. Dismantling the rear axle had shown up that one of the 16-leaf rear springs had 14 leaves, the other 15, one of them broken. Buses at that time sometimes did have uneven springs to counter the effect of the road camber and the Olympic indeed has such a feature: but should have it only at the front, not the rear.

a pivotal problem & panel precision

Back in 2009, a very neat pedal fulcrum block had been made up and put in place. This led to fun and games. Bolts had been made up to attach it to the chassis. A smaller fulcrum block takes the accelerator linkage and brake valve, but no-one could find where that bolted on. The problem was compounded by the fact they discovered that when these linkages looked right, they wouldn't connect to anything and eventually they were taken part again and reassembled upside down. That worked, and it became apparent that bolts for the pedal fulcrum in fact needed to go right through the chassis member with the other fulcrum bolted upside down under the member by the same bolts as the pedal block. New, longer, ones had to be made up, and now everything was neatly connected up.

There had been some progress on the bodywork. All the restored ceiling panels were in place, bar a couple at the front end, left out until the door gear had been sorted. New wires dangled out of the holes where the light fittings would be going. A badly rotted cab side window pan had been used as a pattern to make

Above left, in Stephen Morris's words, "All the restored ceiling panels were in place, bar a couple at the front end . . . New wires dangled out of the holes where the light fittings would be going."

And above right there's Barry Thomas again, at work on the ceiling.

a very fine new one, which was now ready to drop in. The cab window itself was made of anodised brass and will probably be discovered intact by archaeologists in a couple of thousand years' time. Meanwhile Chris Kent had made up a new nearside front windscreen pan to replace the well-rotted original.
The glass was a bit ropey: indeed one part of the sliding window was Perspex: and this would have to be replaced. Indeed all the glass would be replaced, to restore the bus's appearance to as new.

Some of the window pans were now back in the bus; oddly they left a strip of the framing exposed, which looked strange but is correct.

All the side panels were put on loosely to ensure that fuel and water filler flaps were in the right place. All horizontal sections of the frame had been replaced, though the uprights were largely original. However, with the aircraft engineering approach to the Olympic's construction being a much more precise art than the usual wood and metal of the time, getting rivet holes on the panels to line up with their counterparts on the frame proved a major headache. The panels, as we've said before, were of an aircraft grade alloy called Duralumin; obviously the name was chosen to reflect its durability and they have been remarkably unaffected by 60 years' wear and tear, pollution and being subjected to Irish peat bogs. They were reused, and the contrast between these and the steel rear corner panels, now delicate filigree, was very striking.

Such was the precision of the construction that the panels simply abut each other, with no panel straps, so there is no room for error. Getting it all back together was going to be a real challenge, and modern rivets all needed filling to resemble the original dome-headed rivets which no longer seemed to be obtainable. Putting the panels back ought to have been one of the easier jobs, but this was a real challenge, given that replacing the horizontals had made everything move ever so slightly: even the odd half-mm was enough to ensure the rivets holes in the panels no longer matched the rivet holes in the uprights.

This was heightened by the discovery that the waistrail moulding, while capping the panels beneath it, simply abutted the panels above without any overlap: if this were not to go back together precisely, water would seep in through the resulting gap and remain trapped at the bottom where the rail overlaps the lower panels. These were certainly not the usual sort of problems encountered when restoring a vehicle of the late-1940s; they indicated just how advanced the engineering of the Olympic was, though with no thought for people trying to restore them 60 years later!

The entrance step would also be a challenge, as the original had long gone. Indeed, putting the doors back was also quite a task. Unlike the rest of the bus, these were made of wood, though with aluminium panels. One door was already back in place. Attempts had to be made to replicate the original entrance steps, and ensure they didn't foul the doors: even the position of the step light was a matter for some debate.

I ventured to ask Ruth Andrews my usual wrapping up question; would the Olympic be ready for the 2012 Olympics? Her reproachful glare was enough: I changed the subject rapidly.

2012 Olympic?

It seemed that FoKAB was about to suffer a major setback. It was about to lose its premises.

Redevelopment plans had given them a temporary, and, as these things go, very comfortable home in premises owned by Stagecoach for 'a year or two'. That was nine years previously, so that now the redevelopment looked as if it were really going ahead, no-one was complaining. Accommodation like that for nearly a decade was something for which many preservationists would give their eyeteeth.

Winchester is not a place awash with affordable premises suitable for keeping a small fleet of historic buses and facilities to work on them. It's not exactly the sort of place where people will welcome with open arms the prospect of neighbours with noisy equipment and large diesel engines, so that restricted the choices to places with suitable planning permission, and when I visited, the then chairman Peter Murnaghan had just come back from viewing premises which were on the pricey side but otherwise pretty good. Except the doors were 11ft 6in high, no problem for an Olympic but rather more a problem for PD2s, Renowns and Atlanteans.

Peter was optimistic; FoKAB had a habit of coming up smelling of roses, though just now those roses were proving a tad elusive. But the prospect of being forced out into the open had concentrated the mind on getting the skeletal Olympic weatherproof, and when I called in for my next update in late-November 2010 I was somewhat taken aback to find something looking very much like a bus.

a slice of Lemon

JAA 708 had progressed in leaps and bounds. Charlie Lemon, who had done odd bits and pieces on the bus down the years, has been signed up to work full-time on it between coach driving and a new job on the Isle of Wight Steam Railway.

Charlie was modest about his abilities. *"It's all my dad's fault,"* he said: Dad had bought a Bedford OB, MYA 525, which had served for 21 years with Wakes of Sparkford. The young Lemon was hooked, and looked after a number of commercial vehicles down the years, ranging from a 1947 Seddon Mk5 artic which had spent a 40-year working life trundling around de Havilland's airfield at Hatfield as an ejector seat test rig, covering only 27,000 miles in the process, to the well-known Epsom & Ewell Shelvoke & Drewry refuse collector. He also had an Atkinson Silver Knight tractor unit, parked next to Norman Aish's Bedford MLC bus: and Norman had provided all sorts of contacts with suppliers which have aided and abetted the progress of the Olympic.

Opposite top shows the gap between the window pans mentioned in the text. It looks odd, you have to agree, but is quite correct.

Opposite bottom Keith Andrews offers up one of the original entrance doors.

Below is Charlie Lemon.

*Top is Bob Smith, FoKAB's resident engineer.
And immediately above is Steve Webster.*

Although Charlie had no professional experience as a bodybuilder, he trained with an aircraft manufacturer, and of course the Olympic's construction owes much to the world of aviation. Modestly, he would admit he's not much of a dab hand with wood, but he obviously knew what he was doing with metalwork and his full-time work on the Olympic resulted in amazing progress. In the past, I tentatively mentioned the Olympic being ready for the 2012 Olympics to project leader Ruth Andrews, mentally preparing myself for her withering response. This year, she mentioned it first . . . it could now happen!

ready to roll

Mechanically the Olympic was now pretty well complete. Last year we had left it with a conundrum regarding its rear axle: whatever its rear axle had been, it certainly never began life on an Olympic, and its mismatch of bits was not promising. All sorts of suggestions had been made: and ultimately all had been rejected. The bus would keep its existing, overwidth rear axle. The broken bits of roller bearing we reported on last year had now all been removed; it seemed the bearing race had been forced into the neck of the axle with unfortunate results. Graham Green had now rebuilt the differential and it now had a new bearing race. Thrust washers had had to be remade and this had held up progress for around two months. The diff cover had been sorted out and the axle was back in place on the bus. However, there was still the problem of the axle being too wide, and this would be minimised by sourcing some narrower wheels. Norman Aish had found two and Bob Smith another, so they were nearly there. Meanwhile, a set of new crossply tyres had been ordered from Tyrebuyer.co.uk, who not only knocked £80 off the price but, as they were for a charity, gave them free delivery.

Some imagination would meanwhile be required to disguise the fact the rear wheels were sticking out a bit (and to make it street-legal) with suitable wheelarches. The wheelarches it came with, quite apart from now being in several pieces, did not do the noble Olympic any favours in the beauty stakes.

Chris Kent had made up a whole new exhaust system, though the bus was still showing a propensity to crack its manifold. A new fuel tank had been fitted, with new hangers, and after some discussion it had been decided to replace the fuel pipes with new rubber ones, though retaining the 'proper' fittings. Conduit had been installed for wiring, but the electrics were still to be sorted out.

The governor had taken a great deal of setting up; the O.600 engine was good but showing a tendency to hunt. However it was now settling down to a nice steady tickover once it was warm. Just to prove it, Charlie started the bus for me. You somehow expect a Leyland O.600 to hunt a bit, but the

Norman Aish

range of revs at tickover was remarkable, even by Leyland standards. However, once it had warmed up a bit it ran like a sewing machine, and with a bit of accelerator bellowed lustily, in great Leyland fashion. All along FoKAB had been advised to leave the engine well alone, and it was sounding fantastic and transmitting hardly any vibration to the structure.

A few months previously the Olympic had actually moved under its own power. There wasn't much room for it to go anywhere, but it did go and everything was working. It was almost certain that it would put in an appearance at the 2011 running day under its own steam - only in the bus station, though: it was not quite ready to go on the road yet.

looking like a bus again

But the great progress had been in getting the panels back on. Now they were there it was hard to believe they were more than 60 years old: the Duralumin had stood the test of time remarkably and for the most part they looked nearly new.

The original side panels have been put back in place and two window pans can be seen, above left. Progress is visible on the front, too, in the picture above.

Goff Prentice is on the left using his grinder. He was a great loss to the team when he died of cancer in 2010.

Here is Charlie Lemon expertly fitting the new lower panels. The extent of the problem presented by the rear corner panels can be seen, with the solution in the form of new replacements apparent on the right.

That's the great thing with this bus; although most of the framework had had to be renewed, the material you see on the finished object is, for the most part, original. Many preserved buses will have been repanelled, but in this case the use of aircraft grade alloy means the material just hasn't corroded and looks almost like new. Back in the previous summer I had come across the remains of a Catalina on the Isle of Vatersay in the Outer Hebrides; that too looked just as it did when it crashed into the hillside in May 1944. It's remarkable material. Nonetheless, some lower lift-off flaps had had to be remade from 3mm aluminium.

Ever since we started the story of this gargantuan restoration, the big question was, would those panels actually fit as they were supposed to? Unlike most buses of the time the Olympic was precision engineered, so much so that there are no panel straps. All the panels butt up against each other, apart from the window pans which strangely leave strips about 1in wide with framework showing through between them.
The fit has to be perfect, and the panels are simply riveted straight on to the metal frame: no wooden fillets, no room to 'bodge' things into place, secure in the knowledge no-one will ever notice. And no panel straps to cover up those little peccadilloes. No, this is a precision-built bus and therefore the same level of precision had to apply to its restoration.

It will come as little surprise to know, it wasn't a case of riveting all the panels straight on and everything fitting perfectly first time. The framework had for the most part been completely refabricated, using remaining bits of frame for patterns. It was never going to fit perfectly first go. Framing had to be adjusted here and there to make it all fit. Remarkably no-one had noticed that a couple of sections of waistrail had been fabricated to a 6½in width instead of 6in, and Charlie lost two days while he had to make up and fit replacements. Some of the waistrail had to be packed out too, where sections were not quite flush.

Front-end corners were altogether too square, and Charlie had to cut out the curved sections and painstakingly weld pieces back to create a larger radius. Meanwhile, rear corner waistrail sections had been fabricated to just about the correct radius, and the next rail down had been fabricated to match . . . except the body tapers inward towards the bottom of the bus, so actually the radii of the two levels are different: again little quadrants had to be cut out and the sections welded back again, in this case to reduce the radius. Rear verticals also had to be reset.

Bit by bit the panels have gone back on, and they did butt up to each other just as they should. All but three of the window pans were now back in, too, and while I was there the cab side window pan and the windscreen were in place and about to be completed. Charlie had to reposition the upright for the front offside corner one inch to the right to get it to fit. The emergency exit door in the centre of the rear was also put on while I was there, and fitted well but wouldn't shut fully.

Front wheelarches were now back in place, but rear ones needed major refurbishment, having been badly worn by rubbing on the rear tyres.

next phases

There were still some major jobs to go, and the materials for them were stored around the bus waiting to go on. Large sections of new flooring were stacked up alongside the bus, the underside painted silver, and Charlie was looking forward to the back-breaking and hand-blistering task of installing it.

Meanwhile, after much searching the interior lining material had been acquired and was ready to be fitted to the interior panels. Apparently the original green material didn't stand up to the unwelcome attention of the schoolkids from the Olympic's regular school runs, and it was soon painted over. Original samples of what everyone assumed was Rexine seemed not to have been all that everyone thought. 1950-style Rexine was no longer available, but it turned out probably to have been Buckram, a book-binding material, which was still made by Ratchfords in Stockport. Whatever, a dark green Buckram was a very good match for the original, even if the original turned out not actually to have been Buckram, and a suitable 25m roll had been bought (at half the price of leathercloth) and was ready to be fitted to the interior panels below window level. Other interior panels had been painted and were ready to go in.

Below is Chris Rule who became a member of FoKAB to work on the Olympic.

Underneath, Keith Andrews is fitting the window frames back into place.

Glass had now started to go in; Peter Murnaghan, who normally worked in Hampshire County Council's public transport unit, was doing a fine impression of a glazier during my visit. The biggest outstanding job however was wiring the bus up.

Batteries were being relocated to underseat boxes on the nearside, just above the engine; the battery compartment in the rear offside corner would be replaced by a useful locker for carrying spare oil and water etc. OK, it was a move away from the original but a pragmatic one: if JAA 708 ends up having to live out of doors, the batteries are in a less vulnerable position. And when the rewiring was undertaken, cable runs were much shorter.

Wiring for the interior lights had been sorted out when the ceiling went back in, and wires were still hanging from holes which would one day be light fittings. But the rest of the wiring needed to be undertaken from scratch: so far there was only temporary wiring from the batteries to the starter motor with a starter button amidships.

It was remarkable how parts were still around. A brand new, unused Simms dashboard panel, complete with Leyland logo, had been sourced from Ray Trigg in Staffordshire, a specialist in obsolete electrical components for old vehicles. Its wiring looked like it came out of the factory yesterday and was all labelled up. It was actually a Tiger Cub spec, with toggle switches rather than pull switches, but it made eminent sense to drop it into place. It's possible someone may be inspired to refurbish the original one day, but that can be done at someone's leisure and replace the Tiger Cub one at a later date rather than delaying the restoration. Such pragmatism may offend the purist, but most of us would be thrilled to see this bus back on the road and wouldn't worry too much about its toggle switches.

Ray was also the source for a voltage regulator, a speedo, headlights and sidelights. Many years previously a pair of unused semaphore indicators nearly got ditched by Tilbury's of Southampton, who were having a clearout; they assumed FoKAB wouldn't be interested, as they were 12volt. But, remarkably, they were just the right length for the bus, and there weren't many of the proper 24v ones sitting on the shelves of Halfords: FoKAB thought they might just be able to step down the voltage rather than wait a lifetime in case a pair of suitable 24v ones fell out of the ether one day!

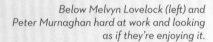

Below Melvyn Lovelock (left) and Peter Murnaghan hard at work and looking as if they're enjoying it.

On the right is the brand new Simms' dashboard panel.

More pragmatism would prevail with lighting. When the bus came back from Ireland it had the remains of flashing indicators at the rear as well as tail and stop lamps. New replacements for these would be fitted, for safety, while the semaphores would also be supplemented by orange flasher bulbs in the sidelamps, for obvious safety reasons. Having been involved in the world of Morris Minors in recent years, it's become clear to me that MoT testers aren't keen on vehicles only having semaphore indicators these days, and not many modern motorists would think to look out for them at the front of a bus they're following.

One electrical problem that hadn't been expected was that the door motor was found to have been burnt out, so it was likely that the Olympic would have to go back on the road with manual doors. The later King Alfred Tiger Cub has a large lever in the cab to work the doors; technology doesn't always move forwards!

Above is the offside semaphore indicator. The additional orange flasher more familiar to modern motorists is visible just behind it.

Left is a drawing of the door mechanism as illustrated in a Modern Transport magazine in January 1950.

Seats obviously would need to be fitted; though built as a 40-seater only 34 came with the bus so at this point it was thought it might end up with a less knee-crushing 34 seats rather than the 40 intended.

One vital factor of the restoration which gave Charlie Lemon much cause for relief was that every component that came off the bus when it was dismantled had been very carefully labelled, so it was immediately obvious to him where it went back. Circumstances are often such that someone else ends up completing the job, so depending on memory for where things go back is not a good idea: and memory has been known to play tricks! One panel however had been a mystery; no-one could work out where it was supposed to go or which way up it was; it was a very odd shape. It turned out to be the rear panel in the cab, which was oddly shaped to accommodate the knees of the front-seat passengers. The ability to seat 40 was a great advantage over the half-cab single-deckers of the era, and obviously Leyland and MCW had to indulge in a little creative thinking to achieve such an aim and give their colleagues in the sales department a competitive edge!

The race was now on to ensure that the Olympic would be in a weatherproof state if the worst were to happen and it had to live out of doors.

ROD TRANSMITTING ACTION TO OPPOSITE DOOR

PIVOTED INTO FIXED CHANNEL

C

ARM PIVOTED

DETAIL AT C

ARM RIGID

B

A

A

B

TRANSMISSION SHAFT

TOGGLE

CLOSED POSITION
OPEN POSITION

TURNING ARM PIVOTED TO DOOR

June 2011
approaching the end of the marathon

One thing the Friends of King Alfred Buses have proved themselves particularly good at over the years has been pulling off a surprise at their annual Running Day. This year, 2011, I wasn't able to get there myself, so when the magazines started appearing with pictures of a pretty complete-looking Leyland Olympic I was fairly gob-smacked. I knew it had been progressing rapidly, but not that rapidly!

I had last seen the Olympic at the end of November, when Charlie Lemon in particular had worked wonders in turning it back from a ghostly skeleton into something that was recognisably a bus, but what appeared at Running Day was virtually a complete bus! So in February I made my way to Winchester again, actually to hear a very entertaining talk by FoKAB's founder James Freeman, who was relating the stories of how FoKAB came to drag wrecks back from far-flung corners of the world and restore them. And at the same time I popped into their secret Central Works, (probably the worst-kept secret in the world!) to see how the Olympic was progressing, and found myself helping to put the windscreen back in.

The top picture shows Charlie and Teresa Lemon working as a team.

On the right is 596 as discovered in the yard of Spirit of '76 Tours Inc. at New Carrolton in Maryland, USA, while above it is on its first appearance back in Winchester on 1 January 1989.

James's thoroughly entertaining talk reminded us that while the Olympic had been back in England for 21 years and was still not finished, their first 'import', a very sad-looking AEC Renown (596 LCG) came back from the States, also pretty well a wreck, in October 1988 and appeared, looking superb, at the 1989 Running Day, less than three months later! That amazing feat set the tone for surprising the crowds at subsequent Running Days. The Renown, it's true, still needed a fair bit of sorting after Running Day, like replacing much of the fuel system and fitting it with a replacement gearbox.

That was nonetheless an amazing achievement, and if FoKAB indulged in a little showmanship, who can blame them? It's been that ability which has set them apart as something special.

So was the appearance of the almost complete Olympic at Running Day a bit of subterfuge? Having seen it just over a month before Running Day I guessed it probably was, and in truth the various trim strips which set the bus off so nicely also covered a multitude of sins, it transpired.

All the time I was recording the restoration of this Olympic, one of the fears had been that with its unusual engineering, it would be difficult to make sure everything married up with the requisite precision. Chris Kent admitted that the job of getting everything straight, to the required tolerance, had been even more difficult than expected. Charlie Lemon had had his work cut out in taking sections apart and realigning them to make them fit properly, and since that Running Day more had to be removed from the bus, straightened up and put back again. So those trim strips concealed parts that didn't line up quite as they should.

Nonetheless a lot of progress had been made in those few weeks: in particular its new glass, in perfectly aligned window pans, was a joy to behold. It also had its new crossply tyres in place, and had genuinely made its appearance under its own steam. That the windscreen hadn't been quite right at Running Day was apparent by the way I found myself doing, for me, a rare bit of hands-on restoration work when I paid my February visit.

Much of what had been put on temporarily for Running Day was now on properly, though the

floor had to come out to have traps cut in it, and was largely back in place. With that and newly-fabricated steps nestling behind doors which were now also in place made boarding it much less precarious than it had been.

Internal window pans were nearly ready for fitting now; some sections had been in place as a trial fit, but they would be painted before they all went in. This is an interesting topic in its own right: after several tries, they settled on a very vivid, almost lime, green. Chris Kent insists it's right, though not everyone is convinced! However an original piece shows that if you imagine it without 60 years of fading, it's probably about right. It will be a talking point on the finished article, and the colour may explain why the window pans were repainted in later life!

Above left you can see the vivid lime green used for the internal window pans.

Above right is floor expert Kevin Lockyer with the part of the new front step.

The services of an experienced coachbuilder working for Hampshire Museums were being put to good use on the wheelarches. It had had none at Running Day, but it now had a neatly tidied-up pair of front ones, which gave the Olympic yet more of a finished look. The rear wheelarches were continuing to give problems, with the overwidth rear axle and the way the wheelarches that came with the bus had been bodged to fit. New ones were to be fabricated and when I saw it the bus was sporting rather splendid boy racer flared rear wheelarches made out of old cornflake packets; sadly these were forming patterns for the replacements and the bus would unlikely be seen in public with these rather fetching adornments. At James Freeman's talk a picture shown of the Olympic when new suggests the wheelarches were originally black, though seem to have been repainted green fairly early on its career.

So despite the rapid progress in recent weeks, there was still quite a long way to go. The whole interior was still to be refitted; most of the original seats came with the bus (though three doubles were missing) but their upholstery was in a poor shape even 20 years ago, and this would be another expensive area to complete. The cab, too, was far from finished. But the Olympic was now weathertight and the end of this massive project was in sight.

July 2012

into the final straight

Well, that would teach FoKAB, or anyone else, not to entrust Morris to do a job that's even vaguely practical! Having triumphantly helped fit the windscreen back into their Leyland Olympic, which was looking more and more like a real bus rather than a Meccano set every time we saw it, of course the windscreen hadn't fitted properly and had had to come out again.

Externally, though, the bus now was looking pretty well complete. All the panelling was in place, and thanks to the efforts of Barry Thomas in getting rid of all the bumps and generally preparing the exterior, it looked pretty straight. All the window pans were in place and glazed, and Bert Brown had fabricated some smart-looking wheelarches to replace the fetching ones made from cornflake packets that it had had last time I looked. They looked the part, though the cardboard ones would have been a nice testimony to King Alfred's endearing ways of make-do-and-mend. However, at this stage a missing upper cab window had been replaced by a piece of plywood, which was probably a more authentic King Alfred style repair than 21st century Kelloggs and Safeway packets. Tempting though it might have been to leave that as a tribute to the good old days, we suspect the MoT people wouldn't have seen the funny side and it would in due course be replaced by glass, to make road junctions a little less hazardous.

The wheelarches were certainly the tidiest the Olympic has sported for some decades, although those at the rear were a tad wider than the originals, as the conundrum of sorting out the rear axle was never finally resolved and the wheels were still slightly further apart than nature intended. At least the axle performed the functions of holding up the back end and transmitting drive to the rear wheels: and probably had at least some origins in the Leyland factory.

The bus also now had its working semaphore trafficators, which seemed enormous and looked as if they could probably do a passing pedestrian a fair amount of damage.

It also now had a pair of doors. These are electrically powered (despite the bus having an air system for its retrofitted air brakes) and took quite a bit of fitting. It turned out that the mounting bracket for one was bent and that for the other was broken, but that had all been sorted out now and the doors fitted nicely. What was surprising was

On the opposite page you can see the wheelarch progress from Cornflake packets to beautifully remade replacements made by Bert Brown. Bert is in big picture at the top, and assisted by Bob Smith bottom left.

On the left is the nearside enormous semaphore trafficator working..

Above is JAA 708 heading for completion - looking like a bus at last!.

how small they were, with a whacking great gap between them: the rubber strip on the edges had not yet been obtained, and you little realise what a huge proportion of the doors is actually rubber until you see them without it.

There has been a wee bit of cheating going on behind the scenes; the original control unit for the doors looked rather like a small electricity substation with copper coils and a rather sad looking spaghetti of old wires and Pete Staples made up a rather swish new one. It doesn't look quite the same, but then no-one very much is going to see it and as it opens and shuts the doors, it does everything required of it, possibly, dare one say, more reliably than Weymann's finest from 1950.

Indeed quite a lot of the electrics have been modernised. It's always a conundrum; old fabric-covered wire and bullet connectors may be authentic, but bus electrics always seem to give inordinate amounts of trouble. FoKAB has developed a technique for rewiring buses using a tray running along the chassis to group all the wiring neatly (and using modern materials), and the Olympic's bodywork electrics have been updated by Pete Staples using the same technique, while Keith Andrews physically installed the new cabling.

While the doors were off the opportunity was taken to fabricate some steps. They look very neat and tidy, and infinitely safer than the inverted milk crate that preceded them, though they are very steep and you wonder how grannies laden with shopping ever boarded buses in the days before DiPTAC. They are also very narrow.

The same could be said of the cab; according to a brochure held by FoKAB the Olympic boasted a 'commodious' cab, a word whose definition has clearly changed since the passing of the Trade Descriptions Act. With the handrails enclosing it in place the driver has to limbo-dance around the handbrake and sharply-angled gear lever, which are both, unusually, on the nearside of the driver's seat, there seems little chance of ever getting out again once you've been shoe-horned into the seat. The steering wheel was missing when I visited, but Leyland was always generous with steering wheel provision in

the hopes you wouldn't notice the weight of the steering. You could hold a sizeable dinner party round one, and once the cab has been squeezed lengthways too, to get 40 seats into 27ft 6in of bus, there really isn't a lot of space for a driver. A rather ropey driver's seat which came from an Atlantean has been retrimmed and looks the part.

The interior of the bus had really come on apace in the last year. The missing seats were replaced by replicas made up by Abacus Tubular Products; possibly a dying skill as buses almost all have individual moulded seats these days. Norman Aish, whose amazing network of contacts came up trumps with sourcing many an obscure part for the Olympic, restored all the existing seat frames.

Meanwhile Paul Toomer, who used to work for H&D Trim, reupholstered the seat squabs with moquette acquired by Tim Stubbs for the restoration of his Rotherham trolleybus. It's not a King Alfred original, but that was no longer obtainable and it certainly looks the part. Lest there be any doubt, the fact that a 1960s King Alfred Setright ticket and a rather older Ultimate ticket were unearthed in the process proves the bus is definitely the real thing (though wouldn't it have been funny if the tickets had turned out to be from Ribble or Isle of Man Road Services?).

Here is Paul Toomer showing off one of the beautifully retrimmed seats

Far left on the opposite page you can see the gap between the newly-fitted entrance doors.

Also bottom right on that page are the newly-completed steps, and above that is the original control unit for the doors.

Above on this page the cab nears completion, although the steering wheel and driver's seat remain to be fitted.

In the meantime, with the wiring complete, Kevin Lockyer had fitted the new floor and Ruth Andrews had covered it with lino. Next, several hundred feet of trim strips had to be laboriously fitted to it.

Meanwhile, the lower interior walls were now dark green, and those vile green internal window pans had also been fitted. They looked vile in isolation and no-one could quite believe they really should be such a vivid lime green: but now they're in situ they blend perfectly with the dark green lower panels and cream ceiling and really look the part: they are quite unlikely to shock any grannies who have managed to heave their shopping aboard.

Melvyn Lovelock had completed the painting of the ceiling, the one part of the bus that gave any hope of it ever being restorable when it first came back from Ireland, and attractive period light fittings set the whole thing off nicely.

Some elusive items needed to finish the bus duly turned up; Ray Bignell at the Ribble Vehicle Preservation Trust managed to find a suitable oil filler cap, though the one item which was still causing problems, apart from a unique style of destination blind, was the electrical control box; FoKAB were still searching for a CAV 189-3 unit for the 24v system. All manner of control boxes had come to light with very similar nomenclature, but it had to be just so: many that seemed close enough were actually for use with an alternator and JAA 708 has a dynamo. An absolute last resort might have been to fit an alternator, but FoKAB described this as 'quite an engineering challenge'; and they are hardly an organisation to be daunted easily by a challenge. Indeed they seldom come bigger than a long-lost Olympic being dragged out of an Irish bog!

and finally . . .

the year of the Olympic

2012 was a momentous and highly successful year for the Olympics: including one in Winchester. At an undisclosed cost likely to be a little over the £15,000 mentioned on page 16, and not quite in time for FoKAB's 1 January 1992 event, JAA 708 will without question be the star of FoKAB's 1 January 2013 Running Day in Winchester.

Having been reported as burnt out, it is now wonderfully apparent that reports of its death were somewhat exaggerated. The Olympic would have floored many a preservation group, but then so would bringing back two sickly buses from the United States and restoring a racing car transporter back to being a coach by the simple expediency of rebodying the thing! Now attention is being turned to creating a safe and secure home for this magnificent slice of Britain's transport history, embodying as it does a significant element of the social history of what had once been England's capital.

Over on the far page can be seen the lovely new floor, and Michael Andrews (representing the next generation of the Andrews family) helping to lay the all-important several hundred feet of trim strips.

On the left is the doyen of vehicle preservationists and one of FoKAB's earliest technical wizzards, Tim Nicholson.

Below, James Bugg wields his paintbrush on the chassis of 708.

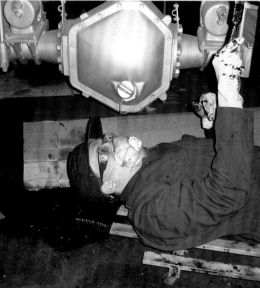

For some years I had been asking Ruth Andrews, coordinator of the restoration of the Olympic, *"Will it be finished in time for the Olympics?"*, risking a tongue lashing or handbagging. It became a bit of a running joke, at least from our end, though at times Ruth's exasperation was palpable. So at the end of my visit on the penultimate day of the 2012 London Olympics, to see 708 in a magnificent splendour not seen by anyone outside FoKAB circles for more than 60 years, she fixed me with a stare and said, *"Well? Aren't you going to ask me?"*

So, what was the answer? A score draw, and with the luxury of a bit of extra time the Olympic could have won. As Team GB picked up its last few medals, JAA 708 was resplendent in two shades of green and cream with black lining out. The interior was resplendent in new moquette and a full set of seats and a complete-looking cab.

It was lacking little. A new destination blind was still in the process of being made up and the destination box was glassless. It lacked the trademark King Alfred statues on the sides, which would be applied the

Opposite, Ruth Andrews is concentrating on a piece of interior corner panelling.

On this page, to all intents and purposes, the inside is now complete.

Compare this picture of the cab with the one on page 51.

following Wednesday. And it lacked an MoT: and at that stage no-one really knew whether it would go, steer or stop. But those few niceties aside, the Olympic marathon was effectively over and every one of the team involved in saving, securing and restoring this magnificent vehicle deserved a gold medal. Team FoKAB had won the day.

What had been left to do since our last visit? Then it had half an interior; now it had a full one. The elusive steering wheel centre had been secured, thanks to Ray Bignell at Ribble Vehicle Preservation Trust. More seriously the problem of the electrical control box had finally been resolved; Tim Nicholson, with several notable vehicle restorations to his credit, had come up trumps using parts of two control boxes supplied by Mark Prescott and the Greater Manchester Transport Society to make one that would work. Finding the correct specification unit had not been possible.

Tim had measured the power output from the dynamo as part of the process, and not been happy with the engine's uneven tickover. He diagnosed a porous diaphragm in the fuel pump, and a partially blocked breather pipe; the pipe would be easy to replace so long as someone didn't mind taking up the floor that had been so laboriously relaid. Nevertheless that wasn't required in the end, thanks to some limbo dancing by John Jowitt and the replacement diaphragm obtained by Tim was duly fitted.

A new sliding window had been fitted in the cab, and while I was there the glass in the nearside bulkhead was finally and triumphantly slotted into place too. We had left the bus with a large gap between the doors last time, and now the rubber seal on both door edges was in place; *"a really horrible job,"* Ruth tells me.

Barry Thomas is on the left, fitting the new sliding cab window, while on the right John Jowitt is blowing through the newly unblocked breather pipe.

And finally, the bus sports a fine new coat of paint, a fetching dark green on the lower panels, a lighter green roof and cream round the windows, ending in a little swoop of muted, almost art deco, exuberance at the rear. Between is a narrow black line, and the aluminium side trims are also picked out in black. After careful preparation work, Jack Parsons came up from Torquay and spent five days brush painting it in situ, in less than ideal conditions. But now the bus had come back to life, a real King Alfred survivor.

On this page you can see expert vehicle painter Jack Parsons rubbing down, painting the first undercoat and applying the final finish to the Olympic.

Over the years Jack, who ran Hampshire Body and Paint at Eastleigh, has painted most of FoKAB's buses.

Two things had caused a certain amount of worry.

First was that apparently cobbled-together rear axle. Chris Kent had made contact with someone from Leyland who confirmed that the dimensions of the rear axle were in fact exactly right. It had looked particularly odd when it came back from Ireland only because it had had the wrong wheels. With the right ones, the back wheels do stand slightly proud, but study of original photos show that to have been the case all along. It seems the axle was right after all.

The other worry is what was described by the advertising people as 'the roominess of the driver's compartment'. With the handbrake oddly placed to the left of the seat, and the gear lever angled back towards the driver, they look for ever in danger of getting inextricably tangled. They also make it look impossible for the driver to get into the cab with a modicum of elegance. And it is. Impossible that is. I tried it and nearly got the gear lever stuck up my trouser leg. Once you're in there, 'roomy' it may not be, but it's not bad. And getting out no doubt gave great entertainment to generations of Wintonians.

During the following week the bus moved out under its own power. An excited FoKAB crew ran it round the yard next to FoKAB's Central Works. James Freeman says, *"The bus sounds truly amazing - a real thoroughbred Leyland roar was to be heard half way round Winchester. It performed well, as far as the limited space allowed - the brakes lived up to their fierce reputation by depositing one of our members on the floor of the gangway when applied hard."*

Once the fun was over,
Bob Smith undertook a dummy MoT test.
This revealed that there was rather more movement in the offside kingpin than even the most generous MoT tester would allow, and Norman Aish sought out a replacement. Unbelievably a new kingpin replacement set, complete with all the bushes, shims etc was obtained and the replacement has now been fitted. It transpires that Leyland kingpins were the same across the entire range for many years.

Meanwhile Tim Nicholson diagnosed a slight control box problem and took it away to fix, and an MoT test was booked for 14 September 2012 which, to everyone's relief, it passed; a major milestone and virtually the final step in a very long journey.

Two significant jobs were done before the MoT: a destination glass and the all-important statues. And there was now no doubt: JAA 708 would be at the King Alfred Running Day on 1 January 2013.

The 'spacious cab' may have been 'spacious' in 1950; either it's shrunk or drivers, like writer Stephen Morris, have expanded...

The main picture records a very significant moment, as the Olympic pauses on the south side of Winchester Broadway, on its return from passing its first MoT test with flying colours.

To remind us that this was once an everyday sight, look at the inset picture dating from the early 1960s.

THE FINISHING TOUCHES

On the far left is the
Olympic badge that was on the front
of Leyland Olympic buses. Note that this one
on the King Alfred bus was silver with a black infill.
If you look back to page 4 you will see a badge with a red infill.
This was the badge that appeared on Olympics delivered to
Isle of Man Road Services and to Ribble, whose liveries were of course red.

On the left Melvyn Lovelock is applying a coat of varnish to the iconic King Alfred
statue emblem, which is what gives King Alfred buses their special appeal. How clever of
Mr Robert Chisnell senior (the Governor) to use the likeness of the great statue that dominates
Winchester Broadway. It showed an understanding of how a strong identity could bring recognition,
as FoKAB is still finding 90 years later.

Above is 708 standing once again under the gaze of King Alfred himself - practising for its first running
day, with a justifiably proud Bob Smith at the wheel. The destination blind was still to be fitted then,
it being hand-made by Geoff Hudspith to match the original, whose layout and style was unique.

A CAST OF THOUSANDS?

Many people have been involved in this massive project down the years. We hope we've remembered everybody.

Many have been identified throughout the book and in the photographs already, but on the opposite page is another fine collection of several of these dedicated people.

If you think you should have been mentioned and haven't please be assured the omission is unintentional and accept the apologies of the authors.

Those that have had particularly significant involvement are:

Norman Aish
Ruth Andrews **7**
Keith Andrews **2**
Chris Kent **4**
Charlie Lemon **3**
Melvyn Lovelock **12**
Peter Murnaghan **5**
Bob Smith **10**
Pete Staples **6**
Barry Thomas

and others who have worked on the project are:

Michael Andrews
Geoff Baker
James Bugg
Eric Chambers
Ray Evans **8**
James Freeman **14**
Brian Gilbert
Colin Godlement **9**
Roland Graves **1**
John Jowitt
John Lemon
Teresa Lemon
Keith Morton **11**
Tim Nicholson
John Newton d.2007
Jack Parsons
Goff Prentice d.2010
Chris Rule
Ken Shackleton **15**
Steve Webster

Parts have been donated by:

Ray Bignell (RVPT)
oil filler cap, steering wheel centre

Colin Billington (via Eric Chambers)
saloon lights

Steve Frampton, Waterlooville
number plates

Mark Prescott (GMTS)
control box, slack adjuster feet, other spare parts, manual

Winchester Community Chest
rivet gun

The restoration was made possible by donations from countless FoKAB members and others, and a grant from Hampshire County Council . . .

and many others whose sometimes quite small contributions made a big impact, like Philip Kirk who produced three original window sliders.

people in the list above with blue numbers are shown on page 64

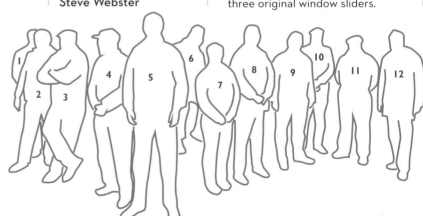

Pete Staples ⑬
James Freeman ⑭
Ken Shackleton ⑮
Chris Kent ⑯

13 14 15 16

Above is the group that went to Ireland on a trip organised and hosted by Tony Leadbetter (bottom left), who was FoKAB's 'fixer' in Ireland. Tony had a marvellous range of contacts and seemed to know everybody in the Irish independent bus world, including Jimmy Glynn. The group stayed in his house before arriving at *the Showroom* and he ferried them about – he also interceded in their very tricky negotiation with Mr Glynn – leading to doing the deal!

As mentioned earlier in this book, Stephen Morris originally told the story of the restoration of the King Alfred Olympic in a series of occasional articles in the pages of Bus & Coach Preservation magazine, to which we are indebted.

This magazine, focussing on the preservation scene, is published monthly and available in newsagents, specialist transport shops or direct from the publisher:

Presbus Publishing
presbuspublishing.com

Classic Bus

Classic Bus is the beautifully designed magazine that helps tell the story of how we got to where we are today.

It's packed full of intelligently written, interesting articles by experts in their field; and illustrated with gorgeous, unashamedly nostalgic pictures.

Published 6 times a year and available from newsagents, specialist transport shops or direct from the publisher.

Subscribe online:

classicbusmag.co.uk

King Alfred buses last ran for real in April 1973. It wasn't very long, though, before two people – initially separately but soon together – started to work on keeping interest in the old company alive. Those two people were Robert E Jowitt (author, and owner of no less than four Parisian buses of the 1930s) and James Freeman. Their efforts had two tangible results. In 1984, after five years of painstaking research, a book was published: *King Alfred Motor Services – The Story of a Winchester Family Business*. The other result, in 1981, was the purchase by James Freeman of Leyland Tiger Cub WCG 104, followed a year later by Leyland Atlantean HOR 591E.

James soon realised that owning and running buses on his own wasn't the right answer, so he advertised a meeting, to be held at the King Alfred pub in Saxon Road. More than 30 people turned up and it was agreed to found the Friends of King Alfred Buses (or FoKAB for short). That was in 1985. A quarter of a century later FoKAB has over 250 members and a fleet of 15 buses and coaches dating from 1931 to 1970.

The buses were collected as they were discovered. Some were easy to find, buy and transport (even drive!) to Winchester, but several have been very major projects: unearthing the buses, persuading their owners to sell them and then getting them back to Hampshire. Two buses came from the USA and, of course, the Olympic came from Ireland! Their Bedford VAL14 coach had become a car-transporter, which made its reconstruction a massive challenge!

In 2000, FoKAB became a registered charity. It furthers its ends of *"increasing knowledge and interest in all aspects of transport heritage"*, with particular reference to King Alfred, by making its vehicles available for use at shows and events around the local area, by taking buses to rallies and, most significantly of all, by its annual Running Day which takes place every New Year's Day.

The first Running Day of all was in March 1983, using just WCG 104. This provided free rides over its old routes, accurately portraying times, routes, tickets, destination displays etc. Journeys started from the time-honoured terminal point by King Alfred's statue in the Broadway (just as they used to do). Each year, the event got bigger. In 1984 there were two buses, and the following year saw the introduction of visiting buses, modelling the operations of other local operators such as Hants & Dorset and Aldershot & District. The switch to 1 January came quickly, after the first couple of years. New Year's Day was chosen because the old buses could have the run of the town (there being no other buses on the road that day). Nowadays, up to 40 buses, with at least 10 King Alfred buses at the core, provide journeys for thousands of visitors from all over the country – even the world! Usually, around 20,000 passenger journeys are counted during the day. Each year, FoKAB tries to produce a surprise for its visitors - or at least something new. So for 2013, the top attraction will without doubt be the chance to see and ride on Olympic JAA 708!

THE FRIENDS

Running Days are FoKAB's main source of revenue. Not that it can charge fares for the journeys, of course. All rides are free – but the various complementary activities, such as the popular Enthusiasts' Bazaar in the nearby Guildhall, sales of a souvenir timetables and many other things, combine to make Running Day an important support for the activities of the Friends.

Otherwise the main source of income for FoKAB is donations (with Gift Aid!) which are the usual way of procuring the major developments that are needed, whether these are acquiring vehicles, restoring them or just keeping them on the road!

If you are interested, the first step is to become a member. So if you have enjoyed the story told in this book, why not consider joining FoKAB? Check this out online at

www.fokab.org.uk
or for further details write to
the FoKAB Membership Secretary
50 Kent Road
St Denys
Southampton SO17 2LH

Thank you!

These pictures illustrate the essence and camaraderie of FoKAB's annual New Year's Running Day with the King Alfred buses supported by up to 30 visiting vehicles.

The unchanging scene in Winchester Broadway provides a perhaps unique setting in which to run the old buses over their old routes.

Indoors, the enthusiasts' bazaar held in the adjacent Guildhall, offers a wide range of books, magazines, models and ephemera. Here Ray Stenning in red, who designed this book, visits the Bus & Coach Preservation stall.

The two black and white photographs on this page were supplied by Melvyn Lovelock. In the upper one JAA 708 was gleaming, and therefore almost new, when it was caught on a private hire job to the Houses of Parliament in London. Note the earlier version of the statue on the side.

The lower photograph is an absolute contrast. It was taken in April 1966 after JAA 708 had been pulled out many months' storage and was waiting to be taken away by Baker West. The destination blinds have been removed and the statue on the side blotted out. In this state, 708 presents a very sorry picture.